Gamers . . . in the Library?!
The Why, What, and How
of Videogame Tournaments
for All Ages

Eli Neiburger

AMERICAN LIBRARY ASSOCIATION
Chicago   2007

While extensive effort has gone into ensuring the reliability of information appearing in this book, the publisher makes no warranty, express or implied, on the accuracy or reliability of the information, and does not assume and hereby disclaims any liability to any person for any loss or damage caused by errors or omissions in this publication.

The paper used in this publication meets the minimum requirements of American National Standard for Information Sciences—Permanence of Paper for Printed Library Materials, ANSI Z39.48-1992. ∞

Library of Congress Cataloging-in-Publication Data
Neiburger, Eli.
    Gamers . . . in the library?! : the why, what, and how of videogame tournaments for all ages / Eli Neiburger.
        p. cm.
    Includes bibliographical references and index.
    ISBN-13: 978-0-8389-0944-7 (alk. paper)
    1. Video games. 2. Computer games. 3. Libraries and teenagers—United States. I. Title.
    GV1469.3.N45 2007
    794.8—dc22   2007010512

ISBN-13: 978-0-8389-0944-7
ISBN-10: 0-8389-0944-2

Printed in the United States of America
11   10   09   08   07   5   4   3   2   1

CONTENTS

FOREWORD

It is midwinter break from school, and my ten-year-old son Michael and four friends are hurrying into the downtown Ann Arbor library for a Pokémon tournament. Clutching their electronic games, they glance around at all the books, CDs, and DVDs as they hustle across the library lobby toward the boldly colored youth room, where all of them made school visits as second graders and where several went to preschool storytimes.

Now in their tweens, the boys head downstairs, past the water jug and snack crackers and into a big library program room that is dimly lit and alive with the music and beeps of electronic games. They find tables, dump their coats, and gravitate toward Eli Neiburger, library technology manager, who since 2004 has coordinated gaming events at the library, most of them on weekends and during school breaks.

In Pokémon tournaments at home, Michael and his friends try to emulate Eli's deep, dramatic voice, taking turns "playing Eli." Eli smiles, greets the boys, and signs them up. All these boys are big fans of the tournaments. As a mother, I'm grateful for the fun, friends, computer savvy, and library enthusiasm they offer my son. It took me several months to reach this point, to become truly comfortable, even enthusiastic, around library videogame tournaments. For me, libraries have always meant one thing: a connection to books. But for my son's generation, they may come to mean books and something more.

To illustrate, in my bag there is a copy of Barbara Lachman's *The Journal of Hildegard of Bingen,* borrowed from the library, of course. As tournament competitors take their seats—one on Eli's right, the other on his left—I am thinking about going upstairs to pick up a copy of James Joyce's *Dubliners* for a book group. Around me, however, boys and girls seem to be experiencing the library in a completely different way, as a cool and fun destination where they might or might not be checking out books. They are greeting old friends and making new ones, and some are stamping their feet in time with the arrows near the console where Dance Dance Revolution is being played. Some are engaged in games on non-tournament game stations around the room.

On my way upstairs, I stop for a moment. Videogame tournaments at the Ann Arbor library? Yes, well, of course. People come here for all kinds of reasons: to see an exhibit of Royal Shakespeare Company costumes, to hear authors of popular knitting books, and to exchange prom dresses. Why not Pokémon battles? For Michael, the events are bringing new pride and confidence. Not only has his videogame "link cable" connected him to new friends, he also has a new library hero (Eli) and career goal (to manage a Pokémon company).

I am enjoying the scene too, talking with parents who are coming and going, returning from upstairs with books or magazines. Some find relatively quiet corners for reading books with younger siblings. Like the children in these families, Michael and his friends are readers. While they may not check out books today, they all read a lot, at school and at home.

Today, though, they are absorbed in Pokémon. They are winning battles, losing battles, advancing into the finals or not. Elizabeth Schneider, a smiling youth librarian, is congratulating winners and offering encouragement to children who have lost battles. The competition is low key, with consolation prizes and mostly happy faces. As the tournament nears the finish, one of Michael's friends is still in the competition. Children are packed around Eli, looking like young geeks-in-training. Everyone is watching with great excitement and energy. And even before this tournament is over, the boys are talking about the next one.

Walking out, I'm an amazed, proud Pokémom. Another mom, a lifelong book lover like me, comments that our kids might use libraries in ways none of us can yet imagine. I nod in agreement. As we pass the youth room, Michael waves to librarian Laura Raynor, who told him folktales in preschool storytimes and who, along with Eli, now represents the library in his young world. I find myself hoping that as Michael and his friends grow up, they will remember just how welcomed and encouraged they felt at this library—home of storytimes, books, and videogame tournaments.

Anne Valentine Martino

INTRODUCTION

My name is Eli, and I am a geek.

I don't remember the day that my dad brought home our Atari 2600 videogame console in 1979, when I was five years old, but I remember asking my mom shortly thereafter if I could take it with me when I left for college. I remember calling every drugstore in town to find a copy of Pac-Man for my Atari, because that's the sort of place you would find such things back then, and I remember my mean babysitter who would plop herself in the playroom with the Atari and not let me or my sister in to play.

I remember receiving a pair of game paddles (joysticks were still optional) for an Apple II computer on my birthday in 1982 and feeling completely dejected and misunderstood because we didn't have an Apple II. (It was waiting in the trunk of the car. Real funny, Dad.) I remember feeling very thankful that adults thought that computers were educational tools, although it turns out they were right. I remember the Apple IIGS I got for my bar mitzvah a few years later and how gleamingly powerful and sophisticated it was (never mind the fact that its every capability and capacity is now dwarfed by my cell phone).

I remember saving my money to buy Nintendo cartridges throughout the 1980s, and I remember spending my science fair winnings on Madden Football and NHL Hockey for the Sega Genesis. I remember taking a trip to St. Louis with my high school friends, where we were devastated to find that we couldn't get my Sega hooked up to the hotel TV. When I left for college, I packed my Genesis and my Atari (which was by then mere nostalgia, my five-year-old self would have been shocked to know). With my purchasing habits freed from parental pragmatics, I proceeded, through the years, to purchase a Sony PlayStation, a Nintendo 64, a PlayStation 2, a Nintendo GameCube, and a Nintendo Wii, all on the days they were launched.

I have a tattoo that consists solely of Nintendo intellectual property.

In short, I'm one of them. You know who I'm talking about. The thumb twiddlers. The cathode-ray zombies. The strung-out junkies who can't even wait for the bus without staring at some sort of a screen. I am a gamer. Videogames are the pastime about which I am most passionate and the products that I most feverishly anticipate. Gaming is also a staple of my family life; I'll often have both kids in my lap and a controller in my hands. My (then soon-to-be) wife completed my collection by giving me a Super Nintendo as a college graduation present. My parents gave my wife a pink Nintendo DS handheld for her birthday. I sing my daughter to sleep with the hymn from the Temple of Time or the waltz from Super Mario Bros., World 2-2. My young son will surely cherish his memories of the first time he camped out with his dad . . . on the sidewalk in front of Toys R Us, the night before the Wii launch.

I've also been earning money with which to support our household gaming habit at the Ann Arbor District Library (AADL) for almost ten years, and I've been managing the technology department there since 2000. I never would have imagined that this job would give me the opportunity to spend taxpayer funds on things like copies of Mario Kart or dance pads, but I have been fortunate to be in the right place at the right time to help videogames become a new and valuable addition to the services that public libraries provide.

We started offering gaming programs at AADL in 2004 in the form of a season of six monthly tournaments for teenagers. We've since added off-season events, events for kids and adults, and all-ages tournaments; we've had Dance Dance Revolution tournaments at outdoor summer festivals, conducted planning meetings and gaming panel discussions with our players, and expanded the service to become a high-profile, intensely competitive part of the lives of our players. We routinely get more than one hundred teenage boys into the library on a Friday night, and we've had players tell us, point-blank, that they never gave a—well, they never cared about the library before these events. We even broadcast the championship events live on cable access, complete with geeked-out player commentary, on-screen leaderboards, and sideline interviews.

The success that we've had with these events is just another facet of the larger trend in libraries to give the patrons what they want. The challenge is that what gamers want can be as alien and arcane to a nongamer as the Internet was during its breakout. And hey, we got through that, right? Uh, hello? Is this thing on?

Like the Internet in the 1990s, gaming is increasingly in demand in every community. Even though it may seem daunting, gaming events and services are within the reach of any public library. All it takes is initiative, and you've shown you've got that by making it this far. Now you just need the advice of a bona fide game geek to help you with the decisions you'll need to make, give you the lay of the land, and point out some best practices to help you get started.

Coincidentally, I just happen to be a bona fide game geek, and I'd like to help you know what you need to know to get a gaming program started at your library, from the planning to the setup to the scoring to cleaning up the smashed pretzels and attempting to get that goatlike aroma of adolescence out of the program room.

I'll start by making a case for games in the library: how they fit into what libraries have been doing for decades and the often surprising demographics of those who include gaming in their leisure activities. I'll then cover some basics of the gamer's world, enough for you to get a foundation of gamer knowledge on which to build your service.

I'll then talk about how to choose game software and hardware and how you can acquire or borrow what you need. Next comes advice about how to plan your events, including a checklist of things to think about along with detailed information about tournament structure, handling crowds, choosing prizes for different audiences, and adding frills to your service as it matures. Marketing and promotion are critical when a library is attempting to reach new audiences, and I'll go over some ideas on how libraries of any size can get the word out.

Then comes game day: everything you'll need to know to answer the questions that will startle you awake the night before the event, such as "How will I keep score?" "How many chairs should I put out?" "What will I do if there's a fight?" and "The which plugs into the what now?" I'll talk about ways to turn your gaming audience into an ongoing community and harness its power for the good of your institution. Finally, I'll offer some resources to take the next steps and get geekier as you go.

So, I'd like to take the next 160-odd pages to share with you my perspective, experience, and knowledge about videogames in libraries and show you why games are a good fit for our institutions, what games you might choose, and how you can produce videogame events at your library that will attract new audiences and gamers of all ages. They are intense events, and they can be very different from what you might have done before, but they are also very warm, positive environments, and fundamentally, they're just not that different from any other library program.

I'm also here as a nonlibrarian (my degree is actually in architecture), and a nearly geriatric representative of gaming culture, to help instill a service perspective that recognizes the public library's historical stigma of uncoolness and its well-ensconced image problems and then proceeds to lay them to waste.

Ready? Press Start.

This Is a Library, Not an Arcade
and Other Entirely Artificial Distinctions

WHY? For the love of dear old Melvil Dewey, why would we take our hallowed houses of learning and sully them with these vile, prurient, mind-rotting entertainments? Well, it's a fair question, as long as you remember that they were saying exactly the same thing about *Pride and Prejudice* not that long ago. Minus the Dewey part, of course.

The answer is simply that public libraries are in the business of meeting communities' content needs, including the content they want only for recreational purposes. Games are content too, and as a format, they are in high demand in your community, especially among those pesky nontraditional library users. So I'll look at some facts (and a few assumptions) about gamers and libraries and examine some of the potential benefits your institution can realize from offering a gaming event or service.

1.1 Facts, Assumptions, Epiphanies, and Resigned Acceptance

Videogames are a big deal these days. In 2005, 228 million videogames were purchased new in the United States for a total of $10 billion. To put that in perspective, 710 million books were purchased new in the United States during the same period for a total of $25 billion. So, the U.S. videogame market is one-third the size of the book market in terms of units and almost half the size in terms of revenue. We could compare that to DVD sales too, but you'd only get depressed about the fact that DVDs outsold books by more than two to one in 2005.

Anyway, gaming is not a niche, at least not anymore. While video-games certainly still have that new fad smell about them, the fact is that the first videogame machines went on the market over thirty years ago, and the kids who played those games, like yours truly, are now parents. According to a survey done by the Entertainment Software Association, 69 percent of U.S. designated heads of household now play some video-games, and the average game player is thirty-three years old, with 25 per-cent of U.S. gamers being over fifty. Gamers are also well spread across genders: adult women (30 percent of gamers) actually make up a larger part of the gamer public than teenage boys (23 percent of gamers)!

Videogames have become a significant—and for many, central—com-ponent of our culture, especially among those nefarious "kids today." For example, 81 percent of Internet-using teenagers play games online. That's a higher use rate than ubiquitous instant messaging and a substantially higher use rate than the things that teenagers are usually allowed to do on the computers at the library (see fig. 1).

This brings us to the biggest piece of the games-in-libraries puzzle: those listless, desultory teens. They're very hard to reach with most library programs and services, either because the events and services aren't appealing to them or perhaps because they aren't willing to risk whatever all-important social standing they've gained by being seen attending an event at the library.

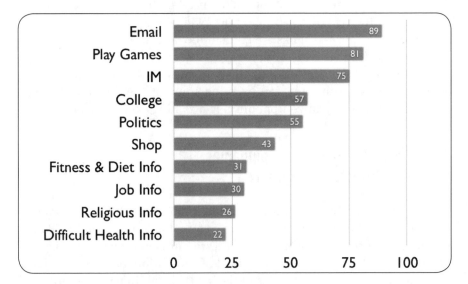

Figure 1

Internet use among twelve- to seventeen-year-olds (percent), from the Pew Internet and American Life Project

While we all have our cadres of dedicated teen library fans (usually the children of dedicated library fans), most public libraries typically reach a very small percentage of the teenagers in their service area. That's not really surprising. If teens steal all their music (and maybe even movies) online, or even download them legally, or subscribe to Netflix, and they have to suffer through *The Catcher in the Rye* for class by Friday, and they think they have all the Google-fu they'll ever need (even if that may not be true), what do they think libraries have to offer them? In their eyes, all our core services have been supplanted by more flexible, better-stocked, more convenient offerings that don't involve shushing, dirty looks, or fussy rules about cell phones.

The bigger problem is that it's not just the teenagers who feel this way. You don't typically see many more twenty-somethings around the library, although they do generally tend to shake off the worries about being seen at the library and come in for stacks of CDs to rip onto their iPods. For many public libraries, there's a yawning chasm between the time that a patron gets too old for Pinkerton (or perhaps Potter) and the time that they have an eighteen-month-old and they're desperate to get out of the house.

At the first-ever Gaming in Libraries Symposium in December 2005, I said, "If you don't offer them something they value now, you're going to be irrelevant to them for the rest of their lives. It's not a risk we can afford to take." That quote was written up on the ALA TechSource blog (along with a dorky picture of my tattoo), and then something interesting happened. One of our AADL gamers found it, and he put that quote into his signature so that it shows up in every comment he makes on our teen blog. He's thirteen, and that comment resonated with him. Of course, his sig had previously read "Eli is awesome," which really resonated with me, but that's OK.

At any rate, while the quote is intentionally dire, the fact is that libraries are teetering on a precipice. Circulation may be doing great (helped along by those CD rippers), libraries that aren't subject to a city council's mishaps may have good (or at least reliable) funding, and our users are utilizing technology to get more out of us than ever before. But who are these users? Are they the same ones we've always had, culturally, economically, ethnically? Our existing audience may be utilizing us better, but that's like preaching to the choir. The issue is that libraries may already have lost a generation or two.

A few months ago, I was doing a local radio interview about our gaming program and other teen services. During the preinterview patter, I asked the host, a woman in her late twenties, if she had a library card or ever used the library. She was surprised that I asked. She already thought that the library had nothing to offer her and assumed that I thought so too. She saw the library as a place for schoolkids, and she didn't see why she would want to go there until she had kids of her own.

Later, after the interview was over, she mentioned that she and her friends were into *Lost* and that she'd been struggling to get caught up with the story because she hadn't seen most of the first season. I said, "Well, you know that the library has the first season of *Lost* on DVD, don't you?" Now she was really incredulous. She simply had not thought of the library in that way.

Obviously, this is a nice little anecdote to prove my point, and if she does have kids and brings them to the library, she might have to walk past the DVD section and receive a whack from the cluestick. But the fact remains that here was a fairly typical twenty-something of mainstream tastes, and when she had a content need, she didn't even think of us. Not for even a second. Not even as she was talking to someone who worked at the library! If we're not careful, the notion that the public library has no value or relevance to modern life (you know you've heard it before) could become the majority view. That's not going to be pretty when the political beast sets it sights on our funding.

Someone who has disposable income and likes to shop typically has very little use for—and probably very little awareness of—what libraries are doing. But wait, it gets worse.

One day, the suits running the content industry, including the record labels, the book publishers, and the movie studios, are going to get their heads out of the sand and realize that they can strike a deal directly with the consumer for hassle-free digital media and sell vastly higher volumes at significantly reduced prices. When that happens, do you think the content industry is going to save a place for the public library in their virtual supply chain? Don't bet on it. Traditional library services exist because the publishers can't currently control what you do with a physical item once you've bought it. Their current plans for digital distribution include the closing of that little loophole. When there's an e-book device that people actually like to use available at Wal-Mart for $30 that has the ability to download and display the latest best seller (or the morning paper) for a nickel per day, our core business could disappear quickly. If you don't believe it could happen, ask a travel agent.

It's important for libraries to stake out turf that our competitors can't touch. Storytime is turf we staked out long ago, and although there has been encroachment from bookstores, our service remains superior in quality and clearly isn't just a sales tool. Similarly, videogame events not only claim unique turf that we can build on, they also allow the gaming community a glimpse of a library that has things that they want and a vision of what we can offer to patrons who have no demand for traditional library services. As the proverbial rug is pulled out from under public libraries, we need to be aggressive in leading the way onto a new heavier rug, with thicker pile and a more contemporary design. People who don't know much about libraries often predict that public libraries will be dead and gone within twenty years, the rotting husks of their musty buildings still filled with copies of *The Cat Who Shat Sequels* and mint-condition phone books while the vibrant physiques of iTunes, Netflix, Amazon.com, and Google stand nearby, whistling and innocently scrutinizing their gleaming cuticles, only occasionally shooting each other dirty looks.

I don't want those people to be right. I don't think you want that either. People who think those kinds of things might not think them after seeing the vibrancy and social power of a gaming event at a library, tying together cliques, castes, and cultures over the camaraderie of friendly competition in a neutral setting. Gaming events at libraries are a relatively easy way to show the disconcertingly large number of people who previously couldn't have imagined what our institutions would possibly have to offer them that we can be relevant to their lives, responsive to their interests, and a place to get something they can't get anywhere else. They might even check out a book, but that's not necessarily the point.

So, tasked with reaching out to this audience that couldn't care less about the library, a teen librarian once came into my office with a simple question. . . .

1.2 AADL-GT, or A Geek's Dream Come True

Once upon a time, there was a library technology manager who really liked videogames. There are probably many such library technology managers—who are we kidding?—but our story is just about this one. Now, his library had recently hired a funky new teen librarian, you know the type, with tattoos and pink hair and a healthy disrespect for sacred cows. This librarian, being aware of the demand for gaming among her target audience and tasked with getting more of them involved, soon found herself in the technology manager's cluttered and toy-filled office, asking him a simple question:

Can we do something involving videogames?

After the manager managed (because that's what managers do) to calm himself down, they started thinking about what exactly they would like to do involving videogames. Should they have a kiosk? It would certainly get used, but it could be a pain to handle, and players could just go to Toys R Us for the same thing. Should they circulate games? They would certainly circulate, but the competition is intense and established, and there's collection development policy, MARC records, and all that to deal with. Maybe someday. Then, the manager fell out of his chair as a big idea hit him in the face.

A videogame tournament. Not just one videogame console, but a network of eight consoles. Not just one tournament, but a season of tournaments that build excitement and audience as they go. Not just a pilot program, but a full-blown series, right from the get-go, to show a teen audience that we not only care about what they're into, but we grok it too. (Do kids these days still grok?)

As you may have already guessed, that technology manager was yours truly, and that librarian was the lovely and talented Erin Helmrich. We had the big idea, now we just needed a bunch of smaller ideas to deliver a cutting-edge service that would knock gamers' socks off (ew, gamer socks) and keep them coming back for more.

First, we set the schedule for the season. We decided on five monthly tournaments, August through December, with the December tournament as the grand championships for the entire season. Winners of each of the first four tournaments would qualify for the grand championships. We also included a wildcard tournament right before the grand championships in December to give walk-in players a shot at the big prizes. We scheduled around local events as best we could (in Ann Arbor, never schedule an event on a day that the University of Michigan football team has a home game) and booked our largest meeting room at our downtown library for all five events.

We decided that our first season would focus on a single game to keep things simple. The choice was obvious, from my admitted fanboy's perspective: Mario Kart Double Dash. There are a lot of reasons to choose Mario Kart (see section 3.2.1 for more), but our biggest reason was not that Mario Kart is enormously fun to play, and appealing to a relatively wide audience, but that it supports eight-station LAN (local area network) play, where eight TVs and consoles link together to make one big race. While this is simple to set up and run, the real advantage here is that right off the bat we could offer players a more valuable experience than what they could have at home, even if they owned the game. Some extra-geeky players might have hooked up two GameCubes together before, but playing a full-speed eight-player race with everyone having their own view of the action is exciting and compelling far beyond the single-player experience.

As we were acquiring the hardware, the promotion began with setting up a teen blog at www.axis.aadl.org. *AXIS* was our newly launched teen newsletter, and we saw an obvious opportunity to build brand awareness and have all our teen efforts benefit from the positive association without having to use the word "library" too much. We made a post about the upcoming tournament series and started to spread the word, with the blog's URL attached. In the spring, our teen librarians always visit the middle school classes in town and get a few minutes to tell students what's going on at the library. This was an invaluable opportunity to get the word out about this exciting new program at the library. There were choruses of gasps and thuds as jaws dropped onto desks when the librarians described the coming tournament season. The teen librarians not only helped get kids excited about the events but also gave them a glimmer of a library that is cool, fun, and relevant. Kids started showing up on the blog with questions, ideas, and excitement.

For each tournament, we wanted to find a way for kids to play a lot at a four-hour event without the risk of being eliminated early, and to wring the most varied play out of the hardware and software choices we had made. We decided to offer three events at each tournament. Players could register for as many as they wanted. The three events were single-player race, team race, and single-player battle. This ensured that even the eliminated kids would be playing again in an hour or so, and the team events encouraged players to work together and keep one another engaged. Each event would have a certain number of qualification matches for each player, and then the top scorers would advance to elimination rounds until we had four winners (or, in the case of team events, four winning two-player teams). In the first and second seasons, there were no prizes for these events; winning an event is how players made it to the prize round.

Our prize budget came from the Friends of the Library. It was a great way for them to directly support service to a group they don't often reach, and it was a good way for the library to avoid spending taxpayer funds on prizes. Each of the four regular-season tournaments had $70, $50, and $30 GameStop gift card prizes for first-, second-, and third-place winners of the prize round, respectively. Our grand championship prizes raised the stakes with an engraved iPod for first place, a then brand-new Nintendo DS for second, and a Nintendo Game Boy Advance SP for third.

We had forty-two players at our first tournament, and attendance grew by about 20 percent per tournament as kids had fun and told their friends. The grand championships had over sixty new players in the wildcard tournament, plus another thirty returning qualified players in the finals.

As the season progressed, the events gained complexity, with our homegrown scoring software passing through a few revisions and our registration process being honed to meet the growing throngs more smoothly. By the time we reached the December grand championships, we had added a Friday night tournament for adults and a Sunday tournament for younger kids, and the local cable access channel broadcast our live video coverage of the Saturday grand championships. They later put a replay of the four-hour event into their rotation, showing it often enough that top players and library staff would be recognized from "that Mario Kart show."

By the end of the first regular season, it was clear that these events were bringing new customers into the library and giving them a very rewarding experience, even if they didn't win any prizes. Parents were happy, teens were geeked out, and we were becoming aware of an entirely new realm of possibilities for highly successful teen library events.

In subsequent seasons, we added new games, reworked the prize structure to have smaller prizes for each event instead of a prize round, and, taking a (web) page from online gaming, we added a "clan" system, where players can form teams of up to six players, and all the points they earn go toward their clan's total score. There's a clan cup final with prizes at the December grand championships, but no prizes for the best clan at each regular season event; regardless, the clan competition is intense and has significantly increased the social interaction at our tournaments.

Our audience now knows what to expect: frequent, professional, high-energy tournaments, conveniently scheduled, with a shot at prizes that they really want. We knew, as the first grand championships drew to a close, that we had to sustain interest and make the next season even better than the first, because all the players simply assumed there would be a second season; they were already making plans about what they would achieve next year.

As the service has matured through its first three seasons, we've found a cycle that works for our players and within our resources, consisting essentially of one three-day tournament weekend each month, with tournaments Friday evening and Saturday and Sunday afternoons. From July to December, Saturday afternoons are slated for teen-oriented grand championship tournaments—still our biggest draw and our longest, most sophisticated events. Friday nights are often adult or all-ages tournaments, and Sunday afternoon tournaments are usually geared toward elementary schoolers. We now offer open play events during school breaks immediately before or after a tournament weekend, when the equipment is already set up.

We've also added new games to the regular- and off-season lineup; Dance Dance Revolution (DDR) has developed its own all-ages audience that has grown into some really great intergenerational events, with more than ninety teens, twenty-somethings, parents, and young kids all having fun together. We also added Super Smash Bros. Melee to our second and third championship seasons (see section 3.2.2), and it's still our single biggest draw in terms of numbers. We've also had a number of one-off tournaments including Guitar Hero, Super Monkey Ball, Madden NFL, and a stand-alone annual event called the Retro Octathalon, where players of all ages have the chance to get high scores on eight vintage (that's pre-1990) videogames. We've also discovered a passion for Pokémon still thriving in the hearts of elementary schoolers with a series called Pokémondays in the summer and a weeklong Pokémania during winter break.

Having tournaments built around a wide range of games has allowed our gaming service to provide something for everyone. We have kindergarteners begging for more Mario Kart events, college students at Friday night Super Smash throwdowns eager to school our uppity teenage regulars, parents delighted to try DDR with their kids, and players in their fifties and beyond socializing, giving the games a try, or just watching their kids or grandkids play.

The biggest benefit we've realized from gaming events is that these teens now care about the library. They know us, they're tuned in to what's going on, and they show up at other events. They've become passionate about the library and the season; they have written a Wikipedia article about the tournament series and argued with the Wikipedians who deleted it as "nonnotable," telling them that our tournaments show that there is "still life left in the library." They've started a fansite for our tournaments where they can argue to their hearts content, and they've invited me to be a moderator in their fan community. They're also asking us how they can get jobs like ours. We mean something to them now, even if they were library users before. As one parent told us, "They used to attend the library like they attended church . . . very passively. You've turned them into explorers, seeking out what the library has to offer, and that, after all, is what you set out to do."

Well, not exactly, we just wanted them to have fun socially consuming content at the library. But this is a nice side benefit.

1.3 Why This Is a Library and an Arcade, or Why an Arcade Is Really Just a Pay-per-Use Noncirculating Collection

I hope that I've made it clear that games are a big deal and that gaming events can offer numerous benefits to a public library, but many people would justly argue that that doesn't inherently mean gaming events belong among a library's service offerings. For example, one of my favorite patron comment cards, received anonymously, politely requested that the library should "Please offer Prostitutes and Pie." Both services would certainly find their adherents, but that doesn't mean they would be appropriate for the organization. Nongamers may look at gaming events much the same way.

Here's why they're wrong. You'd have to dig up the most crotchety children-should-be-neither-seen-nor-heard-espousing stick-in-the-mud to find someone who would argue that storytime doesn't belong in the library (even if they'd prefer that it didn't happen when they were trying to read the newspaper). You're reading books to kids, and libraries are all about books, right? Well, sort of . . . libraries are all about *content*. We circulate content by the ton, and that's definitely our core business (for the moment), but we all know there's more to the library than just content delivery. We've found how beneficial it can be to take the content our users would normally consume individually, at home, and make a social event out of that consumption. We're adding value. Sure, Dad could check out and take home *Who Took My Hairy Toe?* and read it at bedtime, and that's great, but it's even better when parent and child can come to the library together, hear Shutta Crum read it her way, and laugh, smile, and be scared along with other parents and children. The added value is the quality of the storyteller, the distinct, engrossing experience, and the social interaction for kids and parents that at-home consumption of content does not provide.

You see where I'm going with this? Hosting a videogame tournament at your library is just like storytime. You're taking content that players would normally consume at home (usually in the basement on the smelly couch), adding distinct value to the experience, and building a highly social event out of it. This is as traditional as library programs get. It's what we do! The only difference is the format, and I think we all know what happens when libraries don't embrace popular new formats (cough, Blockbuster, cough). Just because we don't have prior experience with this thirty-year-old format doesn't mean that it doesn't belong in our libraries. As a matter of fact, most library mission statements are pretty clear that what the patron not only needs but also *wants* belongs in the library.

We've always struggled (and are still struggling) to balance our collections between what the patron wants and what we want them to want, but many public libraries have discovered the dramatic success that awaits when we embrace the recreational component of our mission and develop our collections in response to demand.

Of course, we all have limited piles of money, from the mountain to the molehill. But if games are what teenagers want recreationally and we choose to spend our money elsewhere, we've decided that their entire realm of content interest is not worthy. Stick a bobby pin in that attitude, 'cause that's the bun talking. As we'll discuss later, videogame events are accessible to almost every library; all it takes is the initiative. Everyone in your service area is already your customer. The question becomes, are you offering them anything that they're interested in? Customers who pay for service without receiving any aren't receiving very good customer service, and if we don't have anything that interests them or if they don't know about things we have that would interest them or if they think the library is the place for drooling babies and newspaper-stick-wielding old men ruled by the shush patrol, well, that's still our problem to solve. The stakes are high, but videogames are a natural and highly rewarding next step in the ongoing project we call the public library.

So, how did we get to this point where something like a videogame event is seen as a nontraditional library service, but things we've been doing for less than a decade are traditional already? Libraries, partially due to our archival nature, are historically resistant to change, and as our bun-sporting public image shows, the patrons have concluded that we're not usually all that with-it. Let's take a moment and look at how far libraries have come to put this newest interloper into perspective.

1.3.1 This is a library, not a place to store stacks of paper.

The first known libraries stored clay tablets bearing cuneiform. Think of the arguments that must have been raised in staff meetings as young upstarts tried to prod management into dabbling in the hot new papyrus that the kids were interested in. You would need to replace everything! Shelving systems intended to support lots of weight would now seem like extravagant overspending. Plus, you may be able to drop a scroll without it shattering itself or your metatarsals, but paper will tear and fall apart at the slightest provocation. This paper stuff is simply not as durable as tablets, and libraries have a responsibility to archive only the most durable materials. Besides, didn't we just go over all these arguments when we migrated our collection to Hittite?

1.3.2 This is a library, not a place where people can just take books off the shelves.

Thousands of years later, clay tablets were gone and forgotten for libraries, but their collections of hand-copied books were of such high value that they had to be chained to furniture to prevent the shrinkage issues (theft) we all deal with today. Many of our cherished library furniture traditions, like the lectern or the carrel, date to this era, allowing books to be used in poor lighting while remaining secure. But some libraries actually circulated books, either with a security deposit or without. You can imagine the fights that must have happened as the pressure to cut the chains grew; it's that balance between archiving and access that we still struggle with today. There is even evidence of an early clash between the city council and those tight-fisted libraries of 1212, as the council of Paris called out the monasteries that still refused to circulate their collections (despite the fact that some of them faced excommunication as punishment for loaning a book), chastising them to remember that lending "is one of the chief works of mercy." That must have gone over well at the department heads meeting.

1.3.3   This is a library, not a collection of fiction.

"The free access which many young people have to [this content] has poisoned the mind and corrupted the morals of many a promising youth; and prevented others from improving their minds in useful knowledge. Parents take care to feed their children with wholesome diet; and yet how unconcerned about the provision for the mind, whether they are furnished with salutary food, or with trash, chaff, or poison?"

Sound like a familiar argument for anyone trying to get videogames into the library? Well, the new content at issue is "romances, novels, and plays," and it's the Reverend Enos Hitchcock doing the complaining in 1790. While those toga-wearing hippies the Greeks (who even had branch collections in the public baths, and you can only imagine what went on there) had already been collecting fiction in their closed stacks for two thousand years, most libraries were deathly serious places with recreational reading not even a consideration.

At some point, someone had to push these institutions to lighten up and embrace content that primarily had entertainment value. That couldn't have been easy for organizations that focused exclusively on learning and knowledge. The people in charge had made their careers by lifting themselves above the petty diversions of the unwashed masses, and they weren't about to start buying that Jane Austen filth or dealing with the barely literate philistines who would come in pursuit of it. You just know that at some point in one such conversation, a staunch nonfictionalist would have deemed *Pride and Prejudice* "barely a book at all."

1.3.4   This is a library, not a place where children learn to read.

Most of the services we now consider traditional have heretical—and relatively recent—beginnings. The first record of a children's library is in Arlington, Massachusetts, in 1835. The idea really started to take off at Carnegie libraries around the turn of the twentieth century, with a suspected first storytime taking place at the Carnegie Library of Pittsburgh, West End, in 1899.

Now, a century later, youth services at a public library are as traditional as it gets—even though there is a persistent element that would prefer that youth (and especially those desultory, rambunctious teenagers) be neither seen nor heard at the library. I guess you could call them traditionalists. At any rate, you can guarantee that the first children's librarian had to answer the "Why?" question several times a day.

1.3.5 This is a library, not a music store.

While sheet music was probably an easier addition to a library collection (it being on paper and not clay tablets), the first librarian to propose collecting or even circulating recorded music probably had a tough time pitching the idea. First of all, why would libraries even consider collecting something as fragile as wax tubes? Plus, most of the music on those Edison cylinders is degenerate. Next thing you know young punks will be crawling all over the place, with their obscene waxed mustaches and ostentatious pocket watches, plugged into those infernal machines, listening to that fraud Sousa and his ridiculous mutant helicons.

1.3.6 This is a library, not a movie theater.

Decades later, with our record collections circulating well despite their popularity with those shiftless beatniks and their goatees, a variety of opportunities to collect and circulate recorded movies presented themselves. Film collections and even circulating film projectors were the staple of the proto-A/V geeks who hung out at libraries waiting for such opportunities. But when the VHS market really hit its stride in the 1980s, libraries were so slow to embrace the format that an entire industry sprang up to fill the vacuum, and we lost a substantial chunk of our business to the private sector that we may never get back. While libraries couldn't catch the VHS wave as easily as a for-profit venture could, especially because first-run movies on VHS routinely cost $89.95 in those days, we also took a detour as we once again turned up our noses at what the patron wanted, driving them to our competitors never to return. Many libraries had VHS collection development policies that specified things like "only educational content" or "only *National Geographic*" or "only *Masterpiece Theater*." There's certainly an audience for that kind of content, but it's the one we already have. As public libraries have begun to jump into the chasm of popular materials for each format, we've discovered bottomless pits of demand that are, well, a little scary. DVD collections in particular have shown us that we can attract new patrons, patrons who never would have dreamed that the library had something to offer them. New formats may be rife with logistical challenges, and they're certainly scary, but they are the key to growth.

1.3.7 This is a library, not a computer lab.

I think we can all agree by now that the Internet is not a fad. We all know libraries that took that position, though, especially in the 1990s, when the Internet was so new and ominous. The interesting thing about offering Internet access at a public library is that even the most casual patrons now expect it; people who would never imagine that the library circulates popular movies probably assume that you can check your e-mail there. A new format that made a major impact on society has been perceived as both the final nail in the coffin and the savior of the public library.

First, the ubiquity and unprecedented access to global information enabled by a web browser is often trotted out by council members or fundamentally tax-averse chambers of commerce as proof that the public library has lost its last shred of relevance and money would be better spent elsewhere. At the same time, citizen access to services is increasingly dependent on Internet access (and even predicated on the use of particular Internet browsers of dubious stability), and public libraries have emerged as the only place where people who can't afford or choose not to have a computer can access such services. Unfortunately, you then get the common perception by the affluent that libraries are only for the poor.

Internet access also carries with it the challenge of inappropriate content, and many libraries have policies or software in place to control the content that is accessed on their computers. However, we don't disregard the entire format because of these content concerns (or at least, most libraries don't disregard the entire format), and the management challenges are primarily because it is so hard to determine what is and is not appropriate or for whom. Plus, politicians are involved, which never helps.

1.3.8 This is a library, not a café.

While our collections have long encouraged lingering in the building, most libraries have policies against loitering. To put it bluntly, ever see a "NO LOITERING" sign at a bookstore? As libraries continue to loosen up (and demand for our "traditional" services, like reference, continues to drop), we've found another new role as the Third Place (not home and not work) for our patrons. That means loitering is encouraged, and purely recreational events and services flourish. Along with this comes the retirement of our old no food and drink rules. Sure, the facilities staff and the book fetishists would prefer that their vinyl floors and ten-year-old Fodor's guides remain unsullied by coffee rings, but allowing food and drink, even—gasp—providing them to our patrons, not only creates a warmer, more relaxed atmosphere but also increases the attraction of our buildings to a new generation that likes to mix work and play. Loitering is what libraries are all about! They should be called "loiteries." Wait, that doesn't sound quite right.

1.3.9 This is a library, not an arcade.

Given our established—and rightfully cherished—role as learning institutions, some people may well say that if people want to play videogames, they ought to go to the arcade. That worked perfectly with popular videos: they went to the video store, and they ain't coming back. Despite our piles of dusty books and our somewhat quaint insistence that content should be good, libraries are all about change and have been so for literally thousands of years. Sure, change comes and goes, but it doesn't look like we've yet reached a change rate peak this time around, so libraries need to bend like a reed and embrace another new format before we lose another generation of potential patrons.

We learned from the great papyrus change that we shouldn't be precious about our formats and should attempt to accommodate new ones. We learned from cutting the chain that we can reach a larger audience and spread more knowledge if we allow valuable items to be unsecured. We learned from adding fiction to our collections that we can have a place in our patrons' noneducational pastimes, and we learned that if we are willing to tolerate the noise, snot, and Cheerio particulates, we can provide meaningful services to children that can affect the course of their lives for the better. We've also learned that content is not just about text and that media doesn't have to be socially redeeming, or even any good, for our patrons to want to consume it. Finally, we've learned that there is a role for us in a Googlified world, even if it's just a place to sit and have a cup of coffee.

Each of these lessons applies to the decision of whether or not videogames have a place in the library, and we can be emboldened by the success of each change in terms of our relevance to, and expansion of, our audiences.

Videogames shouldn't be excluded from the library simply because they're new or because they're just for fun or because they're just for kids or because they're not books or because they're so popular and not all good or because they're sometimes inappropriate. If we didn't offer services for those reasons, there wouldn't be any services left. Videogames are a logical next step for public libraries, especially because gaming, even videogaming, has been in the library for decades! It's pretty silly not to want to get into something that you're already into.

1.4 How Videogames Were Smuggled into Libraries aboard an Oregon-Bound Conestoga

Ever since we came to terms with the recreational component of our missions as public libraries (something that is probably still in progress), there have been games in the public library, albeit usually in such innocuous, comfortable forms that we never would have dreamed they were setting such a dangerous precedent of unabashed fun in a house of learning.

The checkerboard has been a fixture, and almost an expectation, in public libraries for a long time. When I started researching tournaments, the first document I found was written by a guy who, as a teenager, had run a series of checkers tournaments at a children's library in the Upper Peninsula of Michigan. Simple games, purely recreational activities, have a long history in libraries, for both their leisure merits and also their social aspects. Game shelves have become a particular staple of children's departments, and many libraries have been doing board game events for years. You'd be hard-pressed to point out the benefit of learning how to play Don't Spill the Beans, Ants in the Pants, or even the venerable Cootie. After all, don't our children deserve better than to be taught that arthropods wear shoes and funny hats?

Adventurous libraries have tried circulating board games, taking a very patron-focused service perspective and a broad content definition. However, this rapidly became difficult because the Scottie dog would always go missing, and everyone always wants to be the Scottie dog. Even tournaments are not unheard of in the library, although they were usually at the instigation of, and run by, a pushy patron. Libraries have long known the value of a game, including prizes, to attract patrons and encourage participation (especially to get kids reading in the summer, right?).

Later, as those infernal computers began to work their way into our institutions, one of the first things we did with them was allow kids to play with them, as long as they were educational games. Of course, they familiarized the kids with computers and delivered some learning content, but they quickly became one of the beloved features of a youth department, as was evidenced by the screaming, tearstained kids who had to be forcibly dragged away from Oregon Trail. Nate the Great never gets that kind of respect.

Shortly thereafter, many libraries climbed aboard the multimedia boom of the late 1990s, especially since so much of the available content had an educational slant to it. CD-ROMs, on in-house machines and in circulation, gave libraries a taste of how hard it was to circulate digital media because the patron was always reporting it as broken, we'd test it, and it would work fine. While this isn't as bad with circulating console games, it's still a problem and a challenge for any circulating collection of digital media.

Setting aside the fact that videogames are already in the library, the first question that the reluctant manager, director, board, or tinfoil-hat-wearing nightmare patron will usually ask about bringing videogames into the library is what's the payoff? This is an excellent question (and one libraries should ask about even the most sacred of sacred cows), although it is blurred by the public library's lack of a profit margin by which to measure the worth of our existence. While I'm about to make the case that videogame events fit perfectly into a public library's core mission and portfolio of services for now, I'll focus on the payoff.

1.5 The Payoff, and Other Things Grantors Like to Hear About

The most prominent payoff from videogame events in the library is reaching a new audience, getting them excited about the library, and keeping them coming back for more. These events have an enormous capacity to draw new faces into the library, faces that you may well start to see at other library events and, heaven forbid, at the circ desk! While I don't view gaming events as a loss leader (see section 1.8), they can certainly be successful in that role. Gamers may never have thought to make a special trip to the library to get a fresh CD to rip (let's be honest here), but when they're already at the library for a tournament, your collections offer the players a completely new level of convenience. And guess what, they'll probably have to bring that CD back before the next tournament, and then they might check out something else. It's a slippery slope.

A well-organized videogame event demonstrates to this new audience that you not only know what they want and can deliver it but also can give even the geekiest blog-reading, iTunes-downloading, Netflix-subscribing Google-fu master an idea of what the library can offer them and how it can fit into their lives. The next generation needs to feel that the public library has relevance in their world, especially once it *is* their world and they're calling the shots.

Many teen services at libraries focus on the educational components of our missions. This is important, but too often our teen services neglect our recreational mission—simple fun. As a result, our organizational relationships with teens are predominantly pedantic. Odds are, the kids who like school are already coming to the library. But what about the other kids, the ones who suffer through school each day in a fluorescence-induced daze, participating as little as possible and looking forward to the end of each day when they can finally, maybe, get to do what they want? While these kids may not be as ebullient, scintillating, perky, or inspired as their Proust-reading library geek peers, it's their library too, and the last thing they want to do with their free time is read or intentionally learn something. We can bemoan this until our buns fall off, but it's a fact of our culture, and it's not just the teens either.

Offering a videogame event demonstrates to this audience (and the teen Proustophiles too) that libraries can be fun without reservation. It's in our mission. We're supposed to be doing it. If we were supposed to restrict ourselves to offering materials with purely redeeming social qualities and educational value, we'd have to throw out half the collection. Videogame events go a long way to filling the yawning chasm that many patrons see between the time they outgrow storytime and the time they are desperate to find something to do with their eighteen-month-old. The result is a more involved, more passionate library user—one who has just discovered that libraries offer him something that is simply fun, no reading levels or homework help or cursed bibliographies involved. The respect that my team gets from these kids is fantastic, because we are meeting them where they want to be, treating them and their interests with respect, and exceeding their expectations.

Once you have their enthusiasm, you'll get a quality of feedback from them far exceeding the outcomes from a routine teen advisory board meeting attended by two kids. You've shown them that you care about what they want, now they're going to tell you how to do it better. Game services at AADL have evolved rapidly because the players are so engaged and invested in the system. They clamor for the floor at our focus groups, and because they know that I'll consider whatever they say, they say what they think. Simply obtaining such a rapport with such a difficult audience is worth the price of admission.

Finally, one of the most rewarding things about these programs is that the teens' parents are appreciative of the way the library reaches out and engages their kids, turning an activity that the parents may worry about into a positive social experience so that they can feel good about their child attending. We've had some wonderful comments from parents, remarking on the warm, friendly, fun atmosphere at our tournaments, how actively their kids have started to explore other library services, and how amazed they are to see their child get themselves up, showered, and out the door to go to the library on a summer afternoon.

One mom told us that one summer day, when her son got himself up and out the door early (by noon) and told her he was going to the library, she didn't believe him. He had to show her the event on our website before she was willing to believe that he was actually going to the library. What does it say about our public image, that the mother of a teenager who says he's going to the library accuses him of lying? Her shock at the reality is priceless. That's the payoff—proving relevance where it had previously been inconceivable to all involved.

1.6 Why Games Are Good for You, or Why You Should Hope Your Surgeon Plays Super Monkey Ball

Not only are gaming events beneficial to your library, they also offer cognitive, social, and educational benefits to your patrons. There is a common misperception that videogames rot the mind; in actuality it is quite the reverse. A wonderful example is a study that showed surgeons who play videogames three hours a week perform laparoscopic surgery 27 percent faster—and make 37 percent fewer errors—than their nongamer peers. The game used in the study was not some intense surgery simulator—it was Super Monkey Ball. Not exactly evidence of brain rot.

Nongamers may see videogames as the mortal enemy of reading and be of the opinion that there can be only one. This ignores the significant amounts of reading that most games require, not to mention all the chatter, FAQs, fan fiction, and other reading and writing that gamers do surrounding the games they love. Games require literacy, and not just reading text but a new kind of literacy that involves information processing, pattern recognition, multitasking, physical coordination, and other cognitive skills that are increasingly valuable in our multithreaded society. The mom of a young gamer once came to one of our programs just to get some perspective on this whole frighteningly alien gaming thing. She was worried that her son was on the computer for six hours a day, with all these windows open, doing five things at once, chatting, reading websites, playing games. "Sounds like a typical day at the office for me," I said. After talking to some of our players and getting a better idea of what it was all about, she said she felt very different about her son's pastime. She hadn't connected his activities to the skills and competencies he might need to succeed in a twenty-first-century workplace and hadn't realized the social component of what appeared to her to be a reclusive activity.

In addition to the cognitive and vocational benefits of playing games, videogame events can meet many of the developmental needs of young kids and teenagers. Many people in library youth services are familiar with the Search Institute's developmental assets: a list of forty "building blocks of healthy development that help young people grow up healthy, caring, and responsible." Sounds like a lofty, worthwhile goal, right?

Videogame tournaments can provide more than twenty of these assets, from receiving support from the nonparent adults who run the events to learning how to peacefully resolve conflict (with your guidance) and becoming more comfortable with players from different cultures, races, or economic backgrounds. Anyone who's ever attended one of our tournaments can immediately tell what a positive, affirming, relaxed, and empowering atmosphere it is for the players, who clamor to participate in the setup, takedown, or production of the event, mix outside their peer group, or just call me by my first name when they've got a question. Videogame events can fill an important need in these kids' lives; they ain't just bait!

1.7 Growing Our Audience, or How I Learned to Stop Worrying and Love the Nonreader

I've heard people say that libraries are here solely to foster learning. I can get on board with that, as long as the definition of learning is sufficiently broad. (Does learning how to wavedash as Dr. Mario count?) I've also heard that libraries are here to share and encourage a love of reading. OK, I can't let that one go by. I agree that books are a core piece of our business, but if you're a taxpayer-funded public library, positioning yourself as a learning institution here to foster a love a reading is going to instantly exclude a wide swath of your paying service population, even in affluent communities. A taxpayer-funded content institution with a recreational component to its mission shouldn't prize one form of recreational content above all others; it is inherently elitist and nondemocratic, no matter how much the printed word has done for civilization over the years.

With all this learning, new literacies, and skill building required of today's citizens just to survive and thrive, they may not have much interest in recreational reading or even learning in general for that matter! There is still a wide swath of the U.S. population that is relieved to have reached adulthood where they don't have to learn anything ever again. It's their library too. It's also the library of the teenager who believes they get nothing out of high school except a diploma and lifelong emotional baggage, and "literature" is just another word for "crap you're forced to consume." They're not going to be too interested in recreational reading at this stage in their lives. Again, you can bemoan it and tsk disapprovingly all you want, but it's *their library too.*

If your community does not already have more gamers than recreational readers, it will soon. We've already found ways to expand our audience and overall circulation just by circulating the DVDs that people actually want to watch (how long is the hold queue for *Brideshead Revisited* as compared to *Over the Hedge*?). Now, there's an opportunity to expand our audience by offering events that people actually want to attend and blotting a bit of the deadly whiff of "educational" off of our institutions. Every library should attempt to offer something for everyone. Gaming events are a great shortcut to reach the vast middle that's not interested in what else you're doing. Offering services to gamers while they are teenagers can make them lifelong library users, and when (if?) they grow up and decide that they might like to read a novel for fun, they're going to head to the library instead of the bookstore.

1.8 Loss Leader or Core Service? Who Cares?

I often hear statements along the lines of "Oh, this is so great, look at all these teenagers actually in the library! Now they can finally discover the staggering genius of Dave Eggers!" I agree that it's great to see teenagers actually in the library, but is their noisy, smelly presence in the building only justified if they check something out—that is, something good? CDs to rip or Japanese comic books or DVDs based on Japanese comic books or magazines about DVDs based on Japanese comic books don't count.

It's a conundrum. Are gaming events a loss leader, like a $20 television at Wal-Mart on the Friday after Thanksgiving—just some otherwise unacceptable bait to get them through the door in hopes that they'll discover something we actually want them to want—or are they an end in themselves? Is it acceptable for gamers just to come to the library to socialize and have a good time? By now you can probably guess my opinion on the issue. Game events are just like storytime: they can certainly function very well as bait, but they have intrinsic value that should not be dismissed just because they didn't get a starred review. Do we say that the only value of storytime is that it gets toddlers into the building? Of course not. That's certainly one of the benefits, but it's not the raison d'être.

Selling your gaming service as a loss leader is a perfectly fine place to start if that's what it takes to get it approved, because just like storytime, your gamers will discover other services that the library has to offer them and become more enthusiastic library patrons. Naturally, it's my hope that gaming events will become as much a self-justified, foregone-conclusion sort of public library fixture as storytime is, to the point where future patrons simply expect to find a good tournament program at their public library. It may sound far-fetched, but it wasn't that long ago that a Wi-Fi hotspot was maybe something you might find on an itchy, strangely named dog. Now our patrons expect it every day, even if they never check out any books. Loss leader or core service? Successful library services should be both.

1.9 Room to Grow, or Just until We All Get Neural Implants and Lose the Ability to Distinguish between Game Worlds and Reality

Nobody ever worries that a library will run out of books to buy (they should, but that's another story). New content is always being produced. Games are no different, except that every few years, the technology landscape is paved over and rebuilt. As the gaming audience continues to grow, gaming events in the library can grow with them. Gaming is gaining in audience and in appeal, and a library that begins a gaming service can rest assured that there will always be new things it can find to shake up and expand its existing gaming audience in multiple directions: to appeal more to older, more casual players or to girls exclusively or to beginning gamers or to parent-child teams where the parent may not be a gamer.

Establishing a gaming service makes a move toward more patron-oriented, responsive service in general, and the nontraditional library users coming into the building may create demand for services that wasn't there before. Tournaments also scale well: they can start small, but they can almost always be bigger, with higher stakes, more events, newer games, or newer takes on older titles. Getting this high-energy crowd through the door and thrilling them is a great foundation on which to continue to build services for the upcoming generations and the disruptive technologies they'll embrace that may (or may not) completely displace the core businesses of the public library.

It's important to remember that you can start small and stay small. Smaller gaming events can realistically be done with no money and little time, especially if you're able to get your community's gamers involved in the production and have some prizes donated. Having a space for the TV and a willingness to invite gamers in to play is truly all it takes to get started. What happens next is up to you.

The question isn't really if you should do gaming events at your library, but when? Will you be riding the wave or chasing it?

Or drowning beneath it?

1.10 What's Involved, or A User's Guide to "Just like Storytime"

"No, Eli!" you say. "I don't want to drown beneath the gaming wave! I want to welcome stinky, uncommunicative teenage boys into my library and encourage them to yell at each other! Just tell me how!" Well, you're almost done with the exposition and ready to move on to the meat.

Chapter 2 introduces the gaming world and how it can be fused with the library world to create a scary monster, and why the monster isn't scary—it's just misunderstood. I'll begin with a summary of the current state of gaming and discuss the pros and cons of the various ways that a public library can offer services to gamers. I'll attempt to convince you that gaming events, especially tournaments, offer the most bang for the buck and have the greatest impact on new customers. I'll also discuss what you need to know, find out, or decide before making your pitch to whomever it must be pitched. We'll also cover some selling strategies and ways to monopolize the conversation, subdue all dissent, and steamroll over any opposition. You'll want to read this chapter if gaming is strange and foreboding or if approval seems unlikely, but you may want to skip it if you're already past that stage and are already familiar with the gaming world and its geeky culture.

Chapter 3 covers the current world of gaming software and hardware (in that critical order), including an introduction to absolute basics for gaming tyros. I'll then look at the major genres of game software and the most high-profile titles in each, including an assessment of how well suited each type of game is for different audiences and settings and a few choice titles you should be sure to consider. I'll then look at the hardware landscape and attempt to make sense of all the marketspeak and fanboy-itis surrounding the choice of which game system and accessories to buy. Finally, I'll offer a few tips on how to acquire game software and hardware within a typical library purchasing environment. You'll want to read this chapter if you've never heard of Master Chief or Samus Aran or if you think that the PlayStation 3 sounds like a good value (sorry, cheap shot). You can probably skip this chapter if you've already decided that Master Chief is not welcome in your community or the director already told you to buy four PlayStation 3s because his son said they were cool.

Chapter 4 will help you plan your event from start to finish, including finding space, arranging furniture, scaling your event to handle crowds of uncertain size, and determining what prizes to award, how to design and run the tournament itself, and how to add frills to your event that increase its value far in excess of their cost. I'll also discuss how to break out of the teenage boy demographic and target gaming events to broader audiences. You should read this chapter if the prospect of staging a tournament seems ridiculously complicated, and you can probably skip it if you already know from experience that running a tournament is ridiculously complicated.

Chapter 5 is all about how to market your gaming events and get the word out to those elusive new audiences, including ideas for cheap or even free ad spaces you may not have considered, style tips to avoid producing dorky fliers, ways to reach fan communities on the Web, the power of a blog to promote and build community around your tournaments, and how to maximize the power of word of mouth to increase your audiences quickly. You should read this chapter if you think that Comic Sans is a fun and kicky font or if you're not sure how to market to people who never leave their dank basements. You can probably skip this chapter if you're not allowed to get involved in marketing at your library.

Chapters 6 and 7 are all about game day. From setup to scorekeeping, from calling the shots to calling the plays, from what to feed them and when to why you mustn't complain about the resultant mess, this chapter will take you through a very busy and fulfilling day at the library for all involved, including how to involve your players and make the whole process easier. You should read this chapter if you've never heard of S-Video or would consider serving popcorn balls in a carpeted room.

Chapter 8 is all about momentum. Once you've got your event series going, there are things you can do to maximize audience involvement and enthusiasm and keep the ball rolling between events. I'll also talk about blogging in detail and how you can harness these simple, often free tools to turn your audience into a real self-sustaining community. You should read this chapter if you're worried about how to convert tournament attendance into "library use," but you can skip this chapter if you already have a vibrant online community of event attendees.

Chapter 9 will point you to some resources that will help you take next steps for any of the areas I've mentioned, including vendors, existing online communities, blogs, and so on. There is a lot more information out there to help you, and you may want a second opinion after reading my admittedly biased pro-Nintendo ramblings.

So, that's where you can go from here. Turn the page and enter the dark and smelly world of the gaming culture.

The Gaming World
and How It Can Be Appropriately Appropriated into the Library World

Like any good culture, the gaming culture has had quite a while to ferment and has worked up a unique aroma. You probably think I'm overdoing it with the smelly thing. You won't think that after your first Dance Dance Revolution event on a summer afternoon. Anyway, what's most interesting about the gaming culture is that while it has its factions, it is a part of daily life for a lot of people, especially young people. Gaming certainly had its geek phase, and it still has its geeky corners, but among modern adolescents, playing videogames in some form is as much a part of their lives as talking on the phone, watching movies, or listening to music; you'd be hard-pressed to find a teenager who doesn't do it. So, if it's such a big deal, what is it? What are they doing? What's hot in the gaming world, and how can we bring it into the library?

First, here's a review of some jargon.

Videogame: a piece of software that is intended to be fun to use.

Console: a game-playing device that hooks up to a TV and plays software, either downloaded from the Internet or on discs. The current products are the seventh generation of game consoles since the business began in the 1970s.

PC: personal computer, which is home to game software of greater complexity and flexibility than game consoles—prone to viruses, incompatibility, shady copy protection schemes, and the infamous blue screen of death.

Graphics: the images that are produced on the screen by game software and an easy way for marketers to convince consumers to purchase their title.

Video card: an interchangeable component in a PC that is responsible for the display of graphics and is occasionally used as an indicator of manhood for the most enthusiastic PC gamers.

Controller: a handheld control device that hooks up to a console either wired or wirelessly and allows the player to control the action on the screen (or hurl it at the screen if they are frustrated or careless).

Memory card: a small data storage device that plugs into a console and allows players to save their progress in a game, which is becoming obsolete as new consoles have hard drives or other storage available.

2.1 Six Archetypal and Entirely Overgeneralized Gamers (with Funny Names So You'll Remember Them)

So, who are gamers, and what do they want? Instead of making monolithic declarations, I'll try some overreaching stereotypes. Here are the archetypical gamers of today, what they're playing, why they're doing what they're doing with their free time, what's hot in their world, and how you can get them through the door.

2.1.1 The Hard-Core Gamer

When you think about gamer stereotypes, this is the guy you're thinking about, and he's almost always a guy. He's really into it. Gaming consumes almost all his free time and every available penny of his income. He owns a gaming PC, at least two and possibly three game consoles of the current generation, numerous gaming relics from years past, and at least two handheld gaming devices. Hard-core gamers represent only 11 percent of gamers, but they account for a full third of all game purchases. Our archetypal hard-core gamer (I'll call him Eliteg33k) probably owns at least ten black T-shirts with completely unintelligible sayings like "1 e4t | \ | 008z 4 8r34 | <f4zt" (I consume inexperienced players for my morning nutrition). This type of gamer is usually into many different types of games but is often most drawn to shooting or fighting games. To Eliteg33k, what's hot is simply whatever's newest. Every good new game is the best game ever; anyone who hasn't downloaded and installed the latest modification to a popular title is hopelessly antiquated; and he knows the release dates and can list the innovations of at least twenty yet-to-be-released

titles. Eliteg33k, like all the previous generations of oppressed dorks, may also be infatuated with "dark" imagery and violence and take delight in fictional depictions of blood and gore, even though they might faint at the sight of the real thing.

While it can be easier to get Eliteg33k through the library door on account of his unrestrained passion for all things gaming, his sky-high expectations and well-ingrained habit of wrinkling his nose at the slightest whiff of game ignorance can make him a tricky customer. He'll have scads of questions and suspicions that you couldn't possibly do it right; but once you show him that you know what you're doing, he'll come to every event you have, usually an hour before it starts, just in case you need any help. However, bear in mind that Eliteg33k doesn't read the newspaper or even watch much television, so it can be a challenge to penetrate his bubble and make that all-important first contact.

2.1.2   The Casual Gamer

With numbers dwarfing the Eliteg33ks of the world, the casual gamer (I'll call her Stephani3) likes to play games and probably plays almost every day but just isn't quite as passionate about it as poor Eliteg33k with his dubious hygiene habits. Stephani3 sees gaming primarily as a social activity and either plays games with friends or to kill time. She might play those games with friends in person or online, and she especially likes games that are descended from board games, card games, or puzzles. She also likes rhythm games like Dance Dance Revolution or Donkey Konga (see sections 3.1.11 and 3.2.3). She may dabble in deeper titles, but she mostly will be found playing games in which a match or round of play can be completed in less than ten minutes. Gaming is a major part of her life but not its focus.

Since the social value of gaming is what motivates her to play, Stephani3 finds hotness in the new social elements of games that she finds fun to play. This can mean better in-game chat or more customizable characters or new ways to play that reward socialization within the game. She just wants to have fun with her friends, and new, better ways to do that will always interest her, provided they don't require geeky acrobatics to get them working.

Stephani3 will have a lot of fun at a library gaming event if you can meet the right conditions: a game that she's familiar with and likes to play (or something easy and quick to pick up), a group of peers for her to socialize with, and, for teenage Stephani3s, an environment she'd be willing to enter without too much risk to her social standing. This last part can be the trickiest, especially with all the Eliteg33ks around; no matter how much Stephani3 likes to play your game, she may not be willing to be seen at your event if it's too dorky.

Stephani3 is not necessarily a teenager; adult women (and men) are playing casual games online in large numbers, and while the social status issue is usually not a concern for them, you still have to offer them that pick-up-and-play fun they're looking for. It's just not worth their time to learn elaborate controls and memorize in-game conventions. It's not that they're not capable of this; of course, they are, but they're not as interested in it as the Eliteg33ks of the world.

2.1.3   The Sports Gamer

If you look at the top-selling videogame franchises so far, Eliteg33k and Stephani3 are the driving forces for the top two (Mario and Pokémon); number three (Final Fantasy) is all Eliteg33k, but number four is there thanks to the discretionary spending of someone new. It's Electronic Arts' Madden NFL franchise, which has sold over 55 million copies across all its incarnations, and it defines videogames for a wide swath of gamers. While games were once just for Eliteg33ks, the rise of the sports gamer (we'll call him Bo) has expanded gaming to a vast, predominantly male, not-necessarily-teenage audience that sees gaming as a way to participate in beloved sporting activities that are otherwise available to him only as a cheering spectator or amateur player.

Bo primarily plays sports games. Football, basketball, baseball, auto racing, hockey, boxing, golf, you name it. He is also very interested in realistic sports games where the sport is attempting to shoot your friends or strangers in the head, but he's not likely to want to play anything too cartoonish or fantasy based. He just really likes sports, usually one particular sport more than others, and he wants to have as realistic a sporting experience as he can on the screen. This is why any innovation that increases the realism or currency of a game is hot to him; an NFL game with last year's roster just isn't as good as one with this season's roster. Also, small innovations in gameplay can mean a lot to him if they increase his feeling of control over the game on the screen; it was a big deal in a recent Madden release when gamers could slam one of the controller sticks in the direction they wanted to shove an opposing player.

Even though Bo's interests are relatively narrow, he is not a casual gamer in any way. Most sports games have notoriously complex control schemes, matches can take up to an hour, and mastery requires intense knowledge of the sport being simulated as well as the players and plays of the chosen team. These games take dedication and study to master, and Bo takes them very seriously.

Getting Bo into the library can be a real challenge. If you'll excuse the generalization, he doesn't really like libraries. Also, his social networks are a little tighter and more closed; he's most interested in beating friends so that he can lord his victory over them for years; beating a stranger or meeting new people isn't as compelling to him.

You may already have a gang of Bos hanging around your library scaring off the Eliteg33ks. If they're already there, and you're looking to give them something positive to do, you may want to avoid some of the Eliteg33k/Stephani3–centric tournament ideas we'll discuss later and give Bo what he wants: Madden or NBA Live.

2.1.4 The Sim Gamer

The simulation gamer is usually a pretty smart feller. He wants a game he can sink his teeth into and play a single scenario for hours or even months. I'll call him Lord Willy (bonus points if you know why). Unlike Eliteg33k, he's not as infatuated with the newness or the latest iteration of classic gaming franchises, and unlike Stephani3, he doesn't usually consider gaming a social activity. Like Bo, he seeks as realistic a simulation as the technology can deliver, but unlike Bo's desire to reach the ideal of a playable television broadcast for a single sporting event, Lord Willy just wants to be god. Omnipresent and omnipotent, he wants a game world that he can make his plaything, perhaps to achieve a goal, but maybe just to play or work toward some abstract ideal.

Some simulations have Lord Willy controlling armies or acting as mayor and city council of a growing metropolis, and others have him controlling a single mundane household or rearing a dog or enormous monster. A new high-profile simulation game expected in 2007 will put Lord Willy in control of nothing less than the entire course of life on a planet, shepherding life-forms from microbes to interstellar civilization.

Obviously, what's hot to Lord Willy is a more detailed, controllable, and robust simulation. More so than any other type of gamer, Lord Willy is prone to settle into a title and play it for years, exploring different scenarios or testing his own ability to recover from disaster. He may still play a game every day that's so old Eliteg33k's PC can't even run it anymore.

Some simulations have multiplayer components, where several gods can fight over a world or attempt to shepherd it together. This can be compelling if Lord Willy can find a worthy opponent, but most of his gameplay is solitary. This can make it challenging to get him to a library event, especially because a single match between two people in a simulation like Civilization III can take hours and hours and hours to reach its conclusion. However, depending on the demand and the resources you have available, it may be possible to come up with a workable event to determine who truly is the best god in your community. Again, because Lord Willy is obviously a control freak at heart, he may not be interested in competing in a contest where he doesn't control all the variables. He'd rather be at home, turning the Roman Empire into a global superpower who stopped the Nazi threat before it even began, only this time without ever building any railroads, just to see if he can do it.

2.1.5 The Role Player

With the relative anonymity of the Internet, the lure to step outside of one's self and be someone totally different in a completely different world is irresistible to some. For the role-playing gamer, the ability to be someone else may be the primary draw of gaming. While many games involve playing a role, role-playing games (RPGs) focus on the role-playing part of the experience, often involving detailed information about the character's skills, abilities, achievements, and property. Many RPGs focus on fantasy or medieval settings, and the role-playing gamer (I'll call her Darkshadow Moonbeamwind) loves to become deeply involved with the fantasy world and the character she portrays within it. While RPGs started out as scripted single-player epics derivative of the pen-and-paper rules of Dungeons and Dragons, the Internet has transformed those single-player adventures into highly social shared game worlds inhabited simultaneously by millions of players killing monsters, plundering corpses, finding treasure, forming guilds, attacking other guilds, weathering schisms in their guilds that create new guilds, and falling in love and getting married (inside the game and out). They also work hard to improve their character, earning skills, collecting raw materials, making and selling products, buying property, building homes, and so on. The interaction with the game world has become incredibly rich, as have the game worlds themselves; some of them have a gross domestic product in real dollars larger than some real countries.

Naturally, this means that these games have become incredibly addictive. Darkshadow Moonbeamwind is characteristically devoted to her online world and her place within it, sometimes at the expense of real-world concerns. After all, these are not games that she can just pause and run to the bathroom; these are persistent online worlds, filled with real human friends that are counting on her. While you may hear stories about people who lose sleep, jobs, or spouses to these games, the fact is that, just like other addictive substances, there are probably RPG addicts in your community who still manage to live normal, productive lives despite their secret. Again, there's nothing casual about these game players: modern RPGs have steep learning curves, complex customs and societal norms, and a whole world of places, people, and things to learn about.

What's hot to Darkshadow Moonbeamwind is usually the next update to her chosen game, be it incremental or substantial. Because online RPGs require such a time investment to succeed, most players pick one and stick with it, either until their interest wanes or they max out on achievements and have nothing left to do. As time goes by, the changes to these games can be major; the game makers can release a small change that creates a new class of characters or resolves an imbalance in the economy with unpredictable consequences.

While the role player may not be concerned about the stigma of entering the library, it's harder to build library events around playing her games for several reasons. First, socialization is such a part of the game interface that getting people physically together to play adds little value to the experience. Also, these games often require powerful computers, fast Internet connections, and many hours to make achievements, all of which combine to make actual gameplay events impractical. However, it is possible to have other events built around these games, like discussions about upcoming changes, contests for character design or stories, movies, or songs written about their characters' achievements, and the like. See section 2.2.5 for more ideas on nongaming but game-related event ideas to attract the passionate Darkshadow Moonbeamwind to your organization.

2.1.6　The Competitor

Superiority has an important place in human biology. I'll leave it at that for now. As a result of this ingrained need, there is a drive, especially among the adolescent males of our species, to express superiority over peers whenever and wherever possible, turning even inherently ridiculous pursuits into serious tests of mettle.

This is a type of gamer who may be interested in many different sorts of games but only wants one thing: to defeat someone else, preferably in front of as many spectators as possible (bonus points when attractive members of the desired sex are present). The ultracompetitive gamer (I'll call him Omegamer) usually favors shooters, sports, or fighting games where victory is indisputable, but you'll find him playing more casual games, which can still be quite competitive, or even trying to wrangle directly competitive situations from the more abstract worth metrics of RPGs.

While Omegamer wants to win in every situation, he's usually driven to seek out the fairest battle scenarios. Despite the possibility that an unbalanced "ruleset" might tilt things in his favor, the greater risk is that it might tilt the other way, and he might actually lose a match to an inferior competitor. Omegamer doesn't mind losing as long as he feels that he was facing a greater power; however, he absolutely cannot bear the thought of losing to a lesser player. This can be a problem if you want to use random elements built into the game to attempt to give weaker players hope. More on that later; it's actually quite a big deal in many games.

Unlike Eliteg33k, Omegamer isn't fascinated by the newest thing because he primarily wants to play something that he's had time to master. Professional gaming tournaments rarely touch new games for this reason; it can take years of training to become adept enough to reach an untouchable pinnacle. Omegamer's ideal is simply to be better than everyone else. So, for Omegamer, the older, more established games are hot; they have burgeoning fan communities that uncover every single possible secret so he can never be surprised and that develop regulation rulesets everyone can agree on to minimize his chances of ever falling to a lesser player. He also has much higher standards of gameplay quality than Eliteg33k or Stephani3, who are willing to try new game ideas even if they don't work perfectly. Omegamer is only interested in a game that has the goods: high quality control, predictable physics, deep gameplay, and most important, no surprises.

As you can imagine, Omegamer is a bit of a mercenary, so if you can get your message in front of him about an upcoming tournament for one of his games, with an acceptable ruleset and a desirable prize, the odds are likely that he'll come to your event. He may even look past your unorthodox ruleset or be unconcerned about any social stigma of entering the building if he thinks that there will be easy prey at the event.

Now, these gamer stereotypes are obviously broad characterizations of traits you'll find in the gaming community. Most gamers are a mix of these generalizations. Also, while these archetypes are based on the teenage incarnations, adult gamers fall into the same categories (with more Bos and Stephani3s and not as many Omegamers or Eliteg33ks) and want the same things from their time spent gaming, with the added angle that they may want something they can do with their kids.

The best gaming services will appeal simultaneously to several of these groups (and age ranges) to both broaden and deepen the appeal and get new faces through the door. So, now that you're familiar with these characters and how their "hotness" sensors can be triggered, I'll talk about some of the ways you can generate a little heat.

2.2 Welcoming Gaming into the Library, or Agar Plates for the Gaming Culture

Now that you can recognize these characters in your community, how can you provide them with games—that recreational content they want most?

What services or products can you offer them that they will find compelling? How can you deliver something unexpected that will break through their preconceptions about the library and meet them where they are? There are several options with varying degrees of complexity, risk, and out-there-ness, also with varying levels of possible payoff. You've probably already figured out what type of gaming service this book focuses on, but let's take a look at all of them so that I can explain why this book focuses on one of them.

2.2.1 Circulating Games: When Cherished Models Attack

Circulating games is certainly a way to reach out to the gamers in your community, and as collections they can be highly successful. However, I don't believe this is the best way to start your gaming services. First, putting games on the shelf doesn't do much to build community among the gamers or between staff and gamers. Some patrons may come in to see the collection, but if they don't like what they see, they're just as likely to walk out, never to return. It can be very expensive to start a good gaming collection, especially when every single potential user of the service will compare it to commercial game rental collections.

Inviting the gamers in your community to view you as a free alternative to Blockbuster can backfire on the library, inviting gamers to make unfavorable comparisons that go beyond the scope or size of your collection. For example, you're allowed to use your cell phone when browsing the shelves at Blockbuster, and the guy behind the counter never bothers to shoot you a disapproving look if you get too loud.

Another concern, especially if you haven't already connected with your teen audience, is the likelihood of significant shrinkage during the collection's first few months. It's a lot easier to steal from us than it is to steal from rental or retail facilities, and if you get game-hungry teens in the building who aren't invested in what you're doing, they can quickly lay waste your collection. That won't be pretty on a progress report unless you set expectations accurately up front.

Also, as we'll discuss in chapter 3, there are several formats of game console on the market, and when you start a game collection, you'll need to choose which formats you'll include. There is no right way to make this decision: every choice alienates a substantial portion of gamers in your community. If you don't circulate games compatible with their game system, you have nothing to offer them. Each additional format you intend to support either increases the cost of the service or decreases the scope of your collection. Neither direction is a good value proposition for the gamers in your community.

There's also the whole handheld issue. If they weren't so dang small, handheld games, with their cheaper prices and lower complexity, would be a good choice for your organization and a good way to differentiate yourself from the big boys who don't usually maintain large handheld game collections. However, it can be pretty challenging to safely circulate something the size of a postage stamp.

There's also the challenge of deciding what titles to buy, just like any other collection. You may intend for your collection just to carry the top sellers or the titles with the widest appeal or maybe some of those obscure sleepers that players might not otherwise have bought or rented. You will probably choose not to buy any Mature-rated titles; you may even choose not to buy any Teen-rated titles to avoid the whole issue of inappropriate content, although that's probably not the best way to endear your organization to a teen audience, and, again, we don't want to be on that side of the Blockbuster comparison.

Finally, if you allow requests on your game collection (and I think you'd be crazy not to since that is an area where we provide superior service to video stores), it may well be that many titles never even hit the shelf. That's not too big a deal in and of itself, as long as you have good promotional materials to help gamers know that the service is still available and how they can access it. Otherwise many potential customers may never even know that they can request videogames for checkout. Libraries are traditionally rich in hidden services that you just have to know about to be able to access.

While a game collection can certainly work, and many libraries are circulating games successfully, it's my opinion that a circulating game collection does not deliver enough bang for the buck, reaches too few players (a single copy of a game can be used by more players in a four-hour tournament than it could in a month of circulation), and does little to change what they think about the library. In the presence of such stiff competition for lending games (competition that we created by not jumping on the VHS boom in the 1980s), we can't be satisfied just playing our part to get content into people's hands. We need to add value to that content, just like we've done for decades with picture books, not just buy it and put it on the shelf. While the notion of a circulating game collection may be more comfortable and familiar than the more nebulous concept of a loud, smelly tournament, a game collection simply doesn't offer the same uniquely compelling draw for gamers as a gaming event. And being able to check out games at the library adds no value for the gamer, other than the value of the rental fee they didn't have to pay.

2.2.2 Game-Related Collections, or Scholarly Works on the Wild Pokémon of the Johto Region

There is a middle ground, of course, that offers something unique to gamers without straying too far out of our comfort zones, and that's to steer some youth collection development in the direction of videogame-related print materials. If you buy Pokémon books at all, you've already discovered a heaping pile of content and a bottomless pit of demand. The elementary schoolkids are so thrilled to see that the library cares about their precious Pokémon that their parents can barely comprehend; just imagine what would happen if you had a Pokémon tournament! I'm getting ahead of myself, though.

If you don't already have gaming magazines among your youth periodicals, there are many of them out there, from *GamePro* to *Nintendo Power,* and it's another solid way to show gamers that you care without really doing anything new. Also, if you do hold gaming events, it's great to have some gaming magazines to spread around the room during the event as a gentle way to promote those core services.

Many Japanese games have related manga (and most manga have related games). An excellent example is the Kingdom Hearts manga, a comic book based on a game series that combines Disney characters with characters from the venerable Final Fantasy series of videogames.

Then there are strategy guides. Much like CliffsNotes for games, they tell players all the secret moves, levels, items, and solutions to the puzzles to help them get to the end of a game. The challenge here is that there are thousands of them, and you'll face similar conundrums as with a game collection when deciding what to collect. One option is to set up a small amount of money and a way to expedite ordering and offer a purchase-on-demand opportunity for gamers, buying strategy guides only on request. That way, you know that you're buying guides for the games that kids are playing, and the gamers will feel that the library is nimble and responsive to their needs.

Whatever you decide, there's plenty of game-related content out there, and getting it into your existing collection should involve a lot less kerfuffle than doing something more out-there would. One note of caution, however: don't develop a game-related print collection and predicate future gaming projects on its success. A game-related print won't really bring new users through the door, and depending on your catalog and display, the collection can easily wind up another one of those secret services that patrons just have to know about. You don't want to be in a position where a naysayer can say, "We bought this strategy guide for this weird game because a kid requested it, and no one else has checked it out. Why would we want to have a game tournament when there's clearly no demand?" You probably know just who would make that argument too, don't you? Darn fuddy-duddies.

2.2.3 The Game Kiosk, and Other Opportunities for Negative Interactions with Library Staff

Another common idea is to offer a game system in a teen room or similar space for gamers just to come in and play whenever they want. In the right situation, this can be great, and a real community of players can coalesce around this available resource, coming into the library every day and monopolizing the machine, shouting obscenities, refusing to leave at closing . . . wait a minute.

While a secured game kiosk is a good way to show gamers that games are welcome in the library, it may turn out to be a very effective way to show gamers that gamers aren't welcome in the library. Managing a scarce open resource like a game kiosk in a public space can be a real service challenge. Most likely, before that machine ever got set up in the public area, there would be a list of rules to go with it, a policy on how to handle problems, a set of approved games, a procedure for signing up, a sheet of expected behaviors in a handy Lucite display next to where it would go, and a taped-up sign that reads, "NO LOUD NOISE OR CELL PHONE USE PERMITTED AT ANY TIME." Now, we usually have our reasons for approaching public service that way, but a game system with a long list of restrictive rules attached to it is exactly what people who don't come to the library would expect to find if they heard that there was a game system at the library. They would probably expect a librarian to hover over them all the time, complete with half-glasses and beshouldered cardigan.

We've got to prove them wrong and offer them something they value that they can't get anywhere else. And the fact is that if they don't want to deal with the library's rules about the game kiosk, then they can go over to Best Buy, Toys R Us, Target, or Circuit City and play a game kiosk with no rules, no ID required, no time limit, no one hovering over them and shushing, and on top of all that, a chance to try the latest games with no restrictions on who plays what. Just like with bookstores and their story-times, we don't want our services to be evaluated against a sales tool and found to be inferior.

Also, setting up a game kiosk for gamers "just to play" is like throwing a bone with a bit of meat on it into a roomful of starving weasels. They're all going to want to get it, they're not going to share, and they're likely to turn on each other. Without the structure of a tournament, turn taking may not spontaneously arise, especially if there are no bonds of community formed between the players and people waiting to play. Whatever game you choose is going to get boring fast, and they're going to want to switch games, probably to something that you wouldn't want them to play. When they can't do it, that's a "the library sucks" moment, or what's known in the business world as a bait and switch. When you're trying to make inroads into a new market, you've got to establish an open and welcoming service perspective and avoid "this sucks" moments whenever possible.

It's very difficult to do that with a game kiosk at a public library. It's not that it can't be done, and it doesn't have to be expensive, but the risk of alienating the very group you're trying to attract is substantial. It could be pulled off if you had enough systems out to meet demand and avoid squabbles or a schedule for which games are out on which days or gamer involvement to help you decide what the rules should be (no easy feat if they're not invested yet). Another exception would be in a school library, where kids are already immersed in a thick system of rules and would be expecting the resources to be tightly controlled.

2.2.4 Browser Games and How to Handle Them, or The RuneScape Menace

On the Internet stations at your library, you have one of three situations: a sign that says "NO GAMES," a filter that attempts to enforce "NO GAMES," or a RuneScape problem. RuneScape is an online role-playing game that not only runs on any web browser without requiring any software to be installed but is also free to play. While the graphics and gameplay are relatively simple, it's got the goods: it's fun to play, offers players an engrossing world to inhabit, and keeps them coming back for more. All the time. Every day.

It's not just RuneScape, though; the Internet is full of games and people playing them. From online social versions of classics like Scrabble, bridge, or euchre (upper Midwest, represent!) to single-player puzzle games and infinite rehashes of the great play mechanics of early arcade games, there are thousands of free games that you can play from almost any web browser.

Now, many libraries have looked at the patron checking their e-mail and the patron playing online chess and decided that one is legitimate and the other isn't. You can probably guess where I stand on that value judgment, but I can understand that when computers are scarce, gamers can quickly make things worse. If they have time to kill (and we all know those patrons who have nothing but), they can park themselves at a station and play all day, and if their time is up, they just get right back in line as long as they're allowed. When everybody has to wait longer to use a computer because Darkshadow Moonbeamwhatever is playing her sixth RuneScape session of the day, it's easy to understand why gaming on Internet stations might get the ax. However, that ax is not so easy to swing: if you attempt to disallow games through filtering or software, you may find that it's almost completely impossible. If you have those "NO GAMES" signs, you might consider how it would look to have a "NO MYSTERIES" sign on each shelf of the fiction collection. These measures may be necessary evils to keep things moving when not enough computers are available, but how can you turn these problems into solutions?

There are a few different approaches. First, try to limit the times or days when the games can be played, so that you're not saying, "Sorry, no games," but instead, "Games are only allowed for the two hours after school" or whatever works for you. It's better than nothing in terms of making gamers feel welcome. Second, make use of computers that might be intended for some other purpose, usually a training center. You may be able to find a way to make your training center available for online gaming one day a week or a few hours a day and steer gamers toward that resource. Providing a time and place can be the first step in building some community with and among your players; if you get all your RuneScapers together in the training center once a week for an hour, it's going to turn into a genuine event before you know it.

2.2.5 Game-Related Events, or I Guess They Can Come in, as Long as They Promise to Learn Something

Even if you're not ready for a gaming event, there are lots of ways that you can produce game-related events that are appealing to gamers. One approach is to have events that embrace the creative side of role-playing games. RPG players often love to write stories and songs or make videos about their characters' exploits. You can provide the training room and have an event where they learn to make videos about their characters or a short story contest for "fan fiction" they've written about the game world of their choice.

Another approach is to have events about making videogames. There are several software packages out there that allow players to make their own simple games or even craft elaborate modifications for existing titles. You can then have a contest for the best level design as voted on by the attendees or even have a tournament within a game they created! These events are a relatively easy sell, and although the software can be complex, it's usually not expensive and is often free. So if you can find someone to teach the class (maybe even you!), it can be a great place to start and a beloved event, especially among the Eliteg33ks.

You can also try game-related lectures or panel discussions, perhaps featuring local people who work in the game industry, professional gamers if you can find them, or even just a panel of local gamers there to argue about the best game of the year. However, these events can be very hard to sell to gamers, even if they're already invested; they're just too much like school.

2.2.6 Open Play Events, or Tournaments Where There Are No Prizes or Scores and the Players Just Take Turns Nicely

If you have all your RuneScape players together in the training center or if you're just making your Internet stations available for gaming for an hour or if you have a game system that you're only going to put out once a week or an hour or day, you're having an open play event. Open play is simply making the equipment, whatever it is, available and designated for gaming for a few hours. Open plays make it clear to gamers that they are welcome in the building and the library intends to offer service to them. While they don't offer the same draw as a tournament and can pose some problems that tournaments usually won't, they are much, much simpler to pull off and far less busy than a tournament.

If you've got enough game systems, you can just put them all out and let the players choose one and sit down. You can load each one with a different game or swap out games for players on request if you've got the time. If you don't have enough game systems, you'll want to choose a game with short matches and set up some way for the players to wait in line.

Some problems can arise when players get tired of waiting in line or bored with the games you've made available. Like a kiosk, they may not default to sharing and taking turns fairly, and conflicts can occur if you're not paying attention. However, this is unlikely as long as you set up a welcoming, inclusive atmosphere and don't hit them with too many rules up front. On that note, whoever is monitoring this event shouldn't just sit there and read a book or do other work. Some of that is certainly OK at an open play, but if you get up just once and wait in line for your turn, you've instantly transitioned from proctor to peer, and that's the best way to get their respect.

You don't need to choose between open plays and tournaments; in fact, they work great together. On school breaks, it's fantastic to do a tournament the first weekend and then a string of open play opportunities during the week while your equipment is still set up. It gives you an opportunity to promote the open play events at the tournament, it gives relationships and rivalries that were established at the tournament a way to continue, and it gives the excitement of the event an outlet when it's all over.

It may be that tournaments are not for you, and open play is just fine. That's great, but be prepared for tournaments to self-organize at your open play events, and be ready to accommodate your players if they ask for a whiteboard to run a tournament or some library swag to use as prizes.

2.2.7   Tournaments, or The Most Fun You're Likely to Have on the Clock, Unless ALA Midwinter Is in Hawaii or Something

OK! You made it! Tournaments are a lot of work and can require complex planning and on-the-fly problem solving. You, or whoever is running the event, may need to sustain a high energy level for several hours and field hundreds of questions from players. However, tournaments are far and away the most effective way to welcome gamers into your library, show gamers that their interests are valued by the library, and prove to gamers that the library can do something cool and relevant to their lives, keeping them coming back for more.

First, as I'll cover in detail in later chapters, a tournament event does not have to be expensive, and even if you buy some equipment, the cost to produce a single event gets cheap fast as you get familiar with it. Compared to the cost of starting a solid circulating game collection, tournament events are a much more cost-effective way to reach a large number of gamers, both in terms of initial purchases, if any, and in terms of staff time once you're ramped up. There's usually one tournament weekend a month at AADL, concentrating the staff time needed and the draw of the events into a few short hours per month. The cost-per-user of an established tournament series can be an excellent value for the library, and if you compare it to the cost-per-user of some of those reference books upstairs, well, you get the idea.

One of the biggest advantages of a tournament over other gaming events and services is that a tournament imposes a rigid structure on the event that the gamers actually want to work within. You get all the benefits of a long list of rules and forced turn taking without any ill will or sending any messages of unwelcomeness. Your tournament attendees will actually bring you suggestions for how the rules could be made more rigid and unyielding. I can't overstate the value of the tournament framework to avoid all the things you might be worried about, from taking turns and cheating to conflict and getting tired of a single game. The tournament format works best when everyone participates, so instead of peer pressure daring the rebellious ones to stand up to authority and make trouble, the peer pressure is to conform, shut up, and play by the rules, so that we can all get on with the next round. It's a win-win if there ever was one.

In addition to the benefits of the rigid structure, tournaments are simply more exciting than an open play or a lecture or a class or a strategy guide or a game you can check out. When gamers come to a tournament, they're a part of something big; they have a shot at glory, fame, and fabulous prizes (never mind that third prize is a library pencil cup). They may succeed, they may fail, but they will likely have more fun than they've ever had at the library, because competition is fun, winning is exhilarating, and they've never seen anything like it. Even though gaming is widespread, only a handful of the most hard-core gamers in your community will ever have participated in a tournament before, and if they did, they probably had to pay to get in. You're back to that added value issue: the other options for gaming events and services all offer some value to gamers of various types, but only tournaments offer such a large value, both the intrinsic value of playing a single fun game with friends and the added value of the chance to beat them when it means something, in front of strangers and possibly even attractive strangers. Gamers may have used the library in the past, but how many can say that they had an exciting, exhilarating, uniquely high-value experience there, centered on their favorite content? If they haven't used the library, they're not likely to come just to check out a game they can borrow from a friend or to attend a class or play a game they can play at home. But an opportunity to defeat an inferior player and walk home with the library's money in their pocket will get new faces through the door, and they'll keep coming back.

Finally, while these other types of events offer some opportunities to build community around your service, nothing compares to the friendships, alliances, rivalries, and bonds that are created at a tournament. Tournament attendees have an intense shared experience on which to build new relationships and to feel the solidarity of a group who for once share the same goal—beat everyone else. I've seen friendships form at tournaments that cross racial, cultural, ethnic, economic, and even language barriers that might not have ever been breached if it weren't for the shared experience of the tournament. The best part is that this community, for once, includes you. You're not the passive observer or the harried disciplinarian; you are the game master, controller of their short-term destinies, and, most unusual, a willingly followed leader. They're at the library because they want to be there, and they're doing what you say because they want to be a part of what you're doing. You may find yourself with an unprecedented level of respect and camaraderie from kids who wouldn't have given you the time of day elsewhere in the building, and all you had to do was hustle and juggle for four months to pull off this ridiculous shenanigan of a mutant library program.

2.3 What You Need to Know to Start a Tournament Series, or Librarian, Geekify Thyself

OK, that last line was overly dire. It's really not that hard to start a tournament series and it's not a mutant program; it just requires some knowledge, like any new pursuit. Your first event may well be overwhelming, but you'll quickly become an old hand, and the gamers in your community who can help you will make themselves immediately available, so you won't be on your own. The biggest challenge can be deciding what kind of a tournament you want to have from among the not-quite-but-almost-infinite range of possibilities for competitive social videogame events. Section 2.4 will sketch out the stuff you'll need to consider, and section 4.1 will then offer specific questions you should be sure to ask yourself and suggest how you might answer them. For now, just know that narrowing down this universe of possibilities should happen sooner rather than later so that you can keep your focus tight and your events easy to explain, and that we'll cover how to plan an event in detail in chapter 4.

Knowing how to make smart choices from within this daunting realm of possibilities can be tricky, especially if you're not a gamer yourself or don't have access to a levelheaded one. If you feel at sea even after consuming all the erudite wisdom contained within these august pages, you'll want to find a trusted group to bounce ideas off of. These can be players you've seen circumventing the filter to play RuneScape in the youth department, colleagues or kids of colleagues, your kids or friends of your kids, or even local college students who you take to dinner in exchange for their feedback on your ideas as you go. The trick is to avoid basing your program on the input of a single Eliteg33k, no matter how accurate he says his perceptions are or how much he claims to know about it or whose kid he is. Most Eliteg33ks are fanboys (more on that later), and fanboys by definition are incapable of fair opinions. Listen to Eliteg33k, but at the very least try to find another Eliteg33k to get a second biased opinion. Once you have some experience, it will be a lot easier to make smart choices, but during the start-up phase, finding some expert help can save you time and avoid nasty surprises.

As you start to determine the answers to questions like software, hardware, audience, and such, you'll need to start thinking about how the tournament itself should be structured. You'll find a lot of concrete details about this in section 7.3, but understanding the conventions of tournament structure, including things like single- and double-elimination brackets, qualification heats, and tiebreakers, is critical to making your events successful and professional. Having a trusted group of gamers to test your ideas against as you come up with them is vital; some tournament formats may sound good in theory but can be stymied by weird idiosyncrasies of your chosen game. Also, you should bear in mind that tournaments may have a fixed capacity or a point in their progress after which time new players cannot be added; unlike most other library events, if a player comes too late, they may not be able to participate. There is more on how to handle this, again, in section 7.3.

While the rigidity of the tournament format is one of its principal virtues, rigid doesn't have to mean formal. Avoid formality in all aspects of your tournament program; don't publish an official set of rules and policies. Keep things verbal when you can and always retain the right to change things if you need to stay on schedule or adapt an event on the fly. While it may seem like it is unfair to keep your cards close to your chest, you're just reinforcing your role as the master of these events with your decision being arguable but final. You'll need to have that authority to break ties or deal with unexpected game events. And you never want to wish that you hadn't written something down that you now want to do differently, because Eliteg33k memorized the whole thing and will throw it in your face. The result of this informality keeps you (or whoever is running your events) inscrutable in a good way, which again just reinforces the players' need to stay on your good side. Keep it informal, and you'll always have the ability to change things at the last minute if you have to. Do it often enough, and they'll expect you to shake things up regularly. More on this in section 8.2.

One last topic you'll need to know is how to resolve disputes fairly but firmly, when to address behavior issues, and what to let go. Problems may come up during the event that can be difficult or unacceptably time-consuming to resolve, like a kid who missed a match ninety minutes ago and might have moved on to the next round if he had not missed his match and it's not his fault because he was in the bathroom because he's not feeling well and OK, I'll stop right there. Sometimes you can do something about these, if another player fortuitously disappears and you can slip Mr. In-the-bathroom into the current round, but sometimes you just have to say, "I'm sorry, but there's nothing I can do about that now," and hope that he doesn't live next door to a board member. This is a skill you'll develop quickly because it will face heavy use as you're starting out, but you need to know that you cannot have a tournament without disappointing all but one person in the room at some point. It's unfortunate and unnatural to our organizations, which usually prefer the everybody-is-unique-and-special angle. But rest assured that even though there may be tears at your events, especially for younger kids, they will be back.

2.4 What You'll Need to Think about, or The Agenda for Your Next Few Available Sleepless Nights

When getting started, you may be chased by the nagging worry that you've forgotten to think about something critically important. As long as you remember to unlock the bathrooms, you ought to be OK. I'll tackle this stuff in detail in section 4.1, but for now I'll touch on the areas that will need some thought and decisions from you (or your boss) while your service is in its formative stages.

2.4.1 *Who and What*

This decision is the germ of your service: who are you trying to reach, and what games will you offer to tempt them? While it's likely and well advised for your first pass to simply be "teens," it's important to keep the focus of the "what" on what games, and not on what game systems, you'll offer them, as I'll repeat ad infinitum in chapter 3. Figure out who your target audience is, and what games they want to play, and build from there.

2.4.2 *Where, When, and How Often*

Once you've decided the who and the what, figure out what space you have available that will be best suited to the event, considering the noise, possible crowds, food mess, odor, setup time, and similar issues. You may have several branches with program spaces to consider, or you may need to figure out how to cram what you want to do into an out-of-the way corner that's all you have to work with. You'll need to think about furniture and layout, where you can have food and where you can't, where your events may easily spill out of their boxes and where they must remain tightly constrained. While the best spaces for a tournament are usually somewhat separated from the rest of the building, you may not have that as an option.

You'll also need to decide when library hours and the availability of your target audience are likely to overlap, or if this is the sort of thing you could have outside of library hours. Be sure to look at other big events that may be happening in town (or on television) that you wouldn't want your event to compete with. For teens or younger kids, always try to offer events when they're on school breaks, even if it's just a set of open play events. AADL has found success with back-to-back tournaments on Friday nights and weekends, allowing us to get several events out of a setup. You can find more about these decisions in section 4.1.

Tournaments can often run long no matter what you do, so always leave room at the end for that to happen. You don't want to have to cut it off and shoo them out before the finals. I consider three hours to be about the minimum amount of time for a good tournament for at least sixty people, although you can have shorter events for fewer people. It basically affects how much each person gets to play during the event: the longer the event, the more matches each player will have time for. On weekends, you may want to consider longer events, in the five- to six-hour range, with several different competitions built in. It's a great way to attract an audience and keep them occupied without the risk of being eliminated early and done for the day.

Finally, never look at this as a one-shot event. This is a service. Will you have events every day for a week once a quarter? One weekend a month? Every Monday? Choose a schedule that your players can settle into and expect, and you'll see solid growth as your series proceeds.

2.4.3 Equipment and Start-Up Costs

While I can't stress enough that you can have videogame events without spending money, if you have some money to spend, you'll need to decide how to spend it. As I'll keep saying, the first choice will be the games you want to buy and the second what game consoles you can buy to play them on. You'll want to be sure to leave room to buy some cables and other accessories that I'll cover in section 3.4. It's important to remember that whatever your start-up budget is, if you make the right choices, you can get a lot of use from that initial investment.

Just for ballpark purposes, $500 will get you started with a few choice games and a console or two to play them, if you already have a TV or projector you can use for your events. That's enough for Dance Dance Revolution and another game or two, a solid start and a foundation for some very successful events.

If you can get together $1,000 to $2,500, you'll be able to buy several different types of games and a few consoles to play them on, depending on whether you go with next-generation or last-generation consoles (more on that in section 3.3). You can also consider purchasing some inexpensive televisions if you need them.

If you have $5,000 to build a tournament kit, you will really be in fantastic shape, and you should be able to buy as many as eight stations, including games, televisions, consoles, and controllers, plus nice dance pads, cables, and maybe even an amplifier for voice or music during your events. This is a lot of money for many institutions, but when you consider how many patrons will use this equipment over its lifetime, it's an excellent value. Besides, isn't that about what a set of *Books in Print* costs these days, and how many patrons use that?

2.4.4 Ongoing and Per-Event Costs

If you are able to spend money on the project, you may wish to consider splitting it into the start-up costs as outlined above, plus ongoing per-event costs. This includes your consumables (prizes, food, drinks, paper products) and staffing costs if you need to cost them out that way or if you'll be hiring an hourly game geek to help. Also, you may want to consider proposing some annual money for new games, replacement controllers, or other upgrades as you go. This certainly isn't essential, but it can be a good idea if you only get to ask for money once a year.

As for prizes, I consider $60 a reasonable minimum for the prize budget for a single event, split into $30 for first prize, $20 for second, and $10 for third. It can be less, especially for younger kids, and it can certainly be more ($40/$30/$20 sure is nice), but you want to avoid being cheap whenever possible when it comes to prizes. Also, if you can scrape up some prize money for a big championship prize, like an iPod or a Nintendo DS or even a console, you will raise the stakes and the excitement even higher.

I'll cover food in detail in section 7.7, but you'll want to offer at least snacks and water at a shorter event and consider offering something more substantial at events that run over three to four hours. Snacks can be very cheap; $30 can go a long way if you buy store brand or go to a warehouse club, but be sure to get twice as many cups as you think you'll need. For those longer events, simply supplement the snacks with pizza. It can be more expensive for large crowds, but pizza can usually be offset by sponsorship or donations.

It will definitely help to arrive at a per-event cost figure (which doesn't include amortization of your start-up costs), especially as you're working through the question of how often to hold events.

2.4.5 Staffing and Event Production

Who's going to work the event and how many people do you need? You'll figure this out as you gain experience, but for many events you'll want two staff members or otherwise responsible adults at a minimum, and you may want more if you're doing complex scorekeeping. However, for simpler events, like Dance Dance Revolution, I've done tournaments with close to one hundred attendees as the only staff member there, so it doesn't have to take a large show of force after you get into it.

Aside from the staffing required for the event itself, there's the setup, which will be very time-consuming at first but will get much faster as you gain experience. Again, this is where there's a distinct advantage to having a space you can monopolize for a weekend: you can set up during the day on Friday, and then you just have to open the doors and turn everything on for the next few events. Don't forget to allow time to break it down and put it all away.

As your service matures and you get to know your players better, you'll find it easier to utilize players to help produce the event and decrease your paid staff needs. There's more on this in section 8.1.

2.4.6 Marketing and Promotion

When you're trying to reach a new audience, getting the word out, especially to people who don't read newspapers, can be a real challenge. Chapter 5 covers this in detail, but while you may not need to budget real money for promotion, be sure to budget some time. Once you get the word out, your audience will grow, but it can be a slow start, especially since the gamers in your community are likely to be predisposed to ignore anything from the library.

If you can put some money toward marketing, try having stickers, T-shirts, or fliers made that will help spread the word more easily rather than having to try to decide what ad buys will reach your desired audience. If you do produce some swag, be absolutely sure that it's not lame!

2.4.7 Online Components

It's not exactly critical that you offer your gamers someplace to gather or give feedback online, but if you don't, your ability to build community among the gamers and between gamers and staff will be significantly decreased. This doesn't have to cost a dime and doesn't need the blessing of your IT department, or even the existence of an IT department. You can have all the online community benefits you need from a free Blogger blog. More on this in section 8.1, but you should be sure to consider how your players can interact online, with each other and with you, how you can get online feedback, and how you can give them fame by posting tournament results and leaderboards on the Web.

2.4.8 Next Steps

Depending on how overwhelmed you may be feeling—on the scale of "don't make me laugh" to "do I really have to do all this?"—you may well want to keep your first events small and expand as you go. Just be sure to plan your phases so that they are clearly intended to help you ramp up the service, not trial balloons on whose success future events are predicated. As I've said, depending on your community, you may be off to a slow start, and you don't want to make it too easy for those who expect your service to "fail" to be right. I recommend planning an initial series of six events, even if they're months apart. You can expand to other audiences like adults or younger kids or start with borrowed equipment and then make purchases when the new fiscal year rolls around. Or you can plan to slowly ramp up the size of your tournaments as money becomes available and you get more comfortable with the production. Just be sure you always have some next steps in mind and always expect that the service will continue. Your director or board wants to see a complete vision to know that this is serious business and something worth doing. The more cohesive and confident your plan is, the easier it will be for them to get behind it.

2.5 The Pitch, or How to Sell It without Someone Mentioning Grand Theft Auto

Speaking of directors and boards, at some point in your early planning process, you're probably going to need to get some approval for this crazy thing you're hoping to do. Getting that approval may be your biggest hurdle, depending on your environment; in fact, you may even be reading this book at home just so that the wrong person doesn't see it on your desk. Fess up, we've all been there.

I'll get right to the sticky wicket: it's likely that your board, director, or staff may be of the opinion that videogames are essentially a degenerate pursuit and that a public library should not contribute to the degeneracy of its population. The press doesn't help by running almost exclusively negative (and usually poorly informed) stories about videogames, focusing on the few undeniably crass and violent titles.

So, the first step to take when selling this program to unconvinced authorities or colleagues is to stake out what kind of software will be involved. The Entertainment Software Ratings Board (ESRB) does a very good job of making it clear on the box of every title which audience that game is appropriate for and why. Most of the awful stories about videogames gloss over the fact that the software involved was rated M for Mature (intended for ages seventeen and up) and was not made for kids in the first place.

It may help to establish that M-rated titles are a niche, not the dominant type: only 15 percent of the games sold in 2005 were rated M, while 53 percent were rated E (for everyone) or E-10+ (for ages ten and up). In fact, there wasn't even an M-rated game in the ten top-selling videogames of 2005 (although there were two in 2006), and the three T-rated (for ages thirteen and up) games in the 2005 top ten were all Star Wars games and received their T rating for realistic depictions of violence against Wookiees.

With a somewhat less degenerate picture of the game industry established, hit them with some information about the cognitive and social benefits of gaming. You can cite the Super Monkey Ball study or read Steven Johnson's fantastic *Everything Bad Is Good for You* or look at some of the work of Constance Steinkuehler and throw out some tidbits to take that "mind-rot" edge off.

Even if your plans aren't yet fully formed, be sure to include in the pitch that you will only do age-appropriate events—E-rated events for everyone, T-rated events for teens and older—and that you simply won't be buying any M-rated titles at all. I'm not saying that M-rated games have no place in a public library, just that declaring them off-limits is a very easy way to definitively sidestep much of the resistance you might encounter.

Some libraries require permission slips before kids can enter a tournament. This is certainly something that you can do to assuage administrative concerns, but the fact is that it's not very customer focused, unless you're willing to look the other way while the walk-in players forge the slip faster than Ferris Bueller. If you keep gameplay on-label (within the game's specified age ranges), the players should no more need parental permission to attend than does each kid who uses safety scissors at a craft program.

Sometimes what it really takes to get buy-in and break through the fear of the unknown is forced tournament participation. At AADL, we had a Mario Kart tournament at our annual staff day during our first season and a Dance Dance Revolution and Karaoke Revolution tournament the next year. These events were a blast for everyone involved, a great closer to a fun, productive day, and a wonderful way to foster familiarity and comfort with something that may have been totally new to much of the staff. We also did a multiplier for player scores based on the number of years they'd been with the organization to encourage otherwise unlikely participants to take one for the team. When I do workshops about games in the library, I always include a tournament based on the sign-in sheet (sneaky, sneaky) so that everyone there realizes that these games are fun, not scary, and a positive experience for all involved.

If you're able to establish that games are not inherently evil and that the youth of your community will be sufficiently protected from the evil that their parents already allow them to play with in their own homes (what do they know?), you may still get hit with the "Just because they want it doesn't mean we should do it / I can't justify taking money away from the book budget to pay for this" angle. Here's where you can make the argument that game events are Just Like Storytime™ and that these events are a natural and beneficial addition to your library's portfolio of service offerings. I've already hit you with my best lines about this in chapter 1, but you'll surely want to collect a few success stories from other libraries (see www.libsuccess.org for more) to show that this isn't exactly uncharted territory.

One thing to consider is that, ideally, this should not even go before the board for approval. This is just not that different from what you've been doing all along. If your director has approved it, she should let the board know that this is happening, of course, but this should no more be a board decision than what book to read at storytime would be. Is *Walter the Farting Dog* OK? So moved.

CHAPTER 3

Software, Hardware, and Other Ware

All right, so either you've got the go-ahead, or you're going skunkworks. That's cool. Now you just need to decide what software and hardware, in that order, you're going to buy, beg, borrow, or borrow for an extended period. Now, in order to properly prepare you to make informed decisions, I could rattle off the entire history of videogames, including the nuances of each generation's hardware and software and the market conditions that selected the winners—just ask my editor. However, history is largely superfluous, as gamers tend to be mostly about the new hotness, with a few notable exceptions that I'll get to shortly.

The most important thing to remember is that similar to the old chestnut about the hole and the drill (you know, nobody needs a drill), nobody plays a game console. What they play are *games!* Those consoles are just game players, no matter how transcendent their respective marketing firms claim them to be. First, I'll cover, in detail, what software is out there that you might consider basing an event around, including how suitable different genres are for different purposes, and some recommendations to help get you started. I'll then discuss the hardware you'll need to produce events around these games, from the game system itself to the cables you might want to have on hand.

3.1 Choosing Your Software, or Why You Shouldn't Choose Your Hardware First

Once you've got the go-ahead, it will be tempting just to pick a console or a few of each and get going! Of course, this can work out OK, but if you make your console-purchasing decision based on what's new, what's hot, or what your players advocate, you could wind up locked into a set of games that weren't really what you were looking for. That's why you should start your purchasing process by deciding what kinds of tournaments you want to have and which audiences you want to reach and then come up with a list of featured software. Looking at that list and considering the platforms for which each title is available, you'll be able to make an informed decision about which console purchase will put the largest number of desired titles within reach.

3.1.1 A List of Dominant Gaming Franchises and Genres, and the Franchises That Are Their Own Genres

Videogame development has become an expensive, complex, and risky business. Most corporations would prefer to avoid projects that are simultaneously expensive, complex, and risky. While software development projects can theoretically be made less expensive or complex, those aren't conditions that you can escape if you're doing business on the bleeding edge. That leaves risk, and just like their counterparts in television and film, the big money people in videogames prefer that their projects follow established success to mitigate the risk of a costly flop. Never mind that the costliest flops are often those that are pale imitators of their predecessors. At any rate, due both to risk aversion and to a market large enough to support some lackluster projects, the videogame software landscape is one of predominantly well-delineated terrain with strong genre conventions, except when those new mutant ideas drop off the tree and shake up everything.

Also, bear in mind that franchises (a set of characters or ideas around which several games can be based) are very attractive to corporations. An established franchise makes for easier marketing, a built-in audience, and often, reduced development costs as the programmers don't have to start from scratch to make a sequel. For fans, purchasing the newest release in a beloved franchise is often a foregone conclusion, and if the fanbase is sufficiently rabid, the new game doesn't even have to be that new. It might not even have to be that good!

Stupendously successful franchises (like Super Mario Bros.) not only transcend generations of hardware, but they can become cultural icons in their own right. As long ago as 1990, Sega's Sonic the Hedgehog (who is now well on his way to obscurity thanks to starring in some famously awful games) was more recognizable to U.S. schoolchildren than Mickey Mouse.

Because gameplay ideas can be easily imitated, smash hit titles will always be imitated. Sometimes the apple will fall much too close to the tree (like Great Giana Sisters, sued right off the market by Nintendo as soon as it was released), but there's often enough room around a particularly lucrative trunk to support a small orchard of clones. This can turn a highly successful franchise into a blossoming genre. The best example of this is Super Mario Kart for Super Nintendo, released in 1992, which not only turned a Mario Bros. spin-off into its own franchise but also launched the hugely successful subgenre of the mascot kart racer. It's now hard to recall a time when any given set of cartoon characters wasn't racing small, goofy go-karts and hurling ridiculous items at each other. Starring in a kart racer is a successful videogame or cartoon character's equivalent to actors or athletes who start a vanity charity or record a hip-hop album.

You can trace most major genres back to their original breakout franchise and its imitators. Computer puzzle games are particularly prone to riffing with only the slightest touch of innovation on established themes; there are still new clones of Atari's thirty-year-old Breakout being released online. It's important to be aware of the franchise landscape of your chosen genre when you're deciding on software; it can help you focus your decisions to be able to tell the dominant title apart from its imitators. The last thing you want to do is base an event around a tepid also-ran.

With this rigid, sharp-edged genre landscape laid out before you, bear in mind that the most successful titles are those that span across or, dare I say, transcend several genres to forge a unique play experience. Um, just because I can't think of any at the moment doesn't mean that they don't exist.

Before I get to specific recommendations for your events, I'm going to cover the genre landscape and make sure you're aware of the different types of games that are out there and how well they are generally suited to different types of situations.

3.1.2   Action and Adventure

Action, adventure, and action-adventure games are usually for a single player and often have a long, linear story that the player advances by completing objectives, or a less structured set of goals that a player advances through by acquiring abilities. Gamers expect it to take at least ten to twenty hours to play through an action-adventure game, but even that's a bit on the cheap side; a good one ought to take a satisfying forty to sixty hours to finish, even without seeing everything.

Pure adventure games are not a good fit for a library event because of their focus on single-player exploration and puzzle solving, but more action titles may well have some countable metric by which players can assess their relative worth, providing an opportunity for a unique event as part of a larger tournament: perhaps seeing who can collect the most of some collectable item in a set amount of time.

ACTION AND ADVENTURE	
Tournamentability	👾👾
Openplayability	👾👾👾
Kids	👾👾👾👾
Teens	👾👾👾
Adults	👾👾
Ratings E	👾👾👾
T	👾👾👾👾
M	👾👾

SUBGENRE	DEFINING FRANCHISE
Platformer	Super Mario
Action Adventure	Zelda
Survival Horror	Resident Evil
Violent Sandbox	Grand Theft Auto
Stealth	Metal Gear

3.1.3   Role-Playing Games

While you could probably classify RPGs as adventure games, they are a distinct enough group to be considered their own species, even though there's a lot of interbreeding going on, if you catch my drift. While almost all videogames have the player playing a role, RPGs are usually understood to be adventure games with a statistics fetish. RPGs almost universally involve player levels that are awarded as the player collects experience points. Games will often require players to spend time earning experience points and leveling up before they can achieve particular in-game goals. This is lovingly referred to as grinding, and the oddly pleasurable yet often repetitive work (hunt, fight, win, hunt, fight, win, incremental ability enhancement) involved is a very poor fit for a tournament.

One exception is the franchise second only to Mario in terms of worldwide total sales: the mighty Pokémon juggernaut. Pokémon, unlike most RPGs, is competitive

ROLE-PLAYING GAMES	
Tournamentability	👾
Openplayability	👾👾👾
Kids	👾👾👾
Teens	👾👾👾👾👾
Adults	👾👾👾
Ratings E	👾👾
T	👾👾👾👾👾
M	👾👾

SUBGENRE	DEFINING FRANCHISE
Classic RPG	Final Fantasy
Pet Battle RPG	Pokémon
Action RPG	Kingdom Hearts
First-Person-Sandbox RPG	Elder Scrolls (Oblivion)
Free Online RPG	RuneScape
Not-Free Online RPG	World of Warcraft

by nature and has had its young devotees slavishly collecting and fighting each other with their oddly named, highly collectible little monsters for over a decade. It's also a pure RPG (under that devilishly hard sell) that delivers a world of daunting complexity and requires far more tactical and strategic sophistication of its players than the elementary audience is usually thought to possess. Pokémon spin-offs allow the battles that players would normally have between their two handhelds to be shown on a big screen with much-improved graphics and sound. Pokémon demand isn't going anywhere; see section 3.2.6 for more details.

Then there's RuneScape. Even if you don't know anything else about gaming, if you work in a library that has Internet access, you probably know all about RuneScape. Many libraries will have dedicated RuneScape players trying to tie up Internet stations, or even policies designed to prevent RuneScape players from tying up the Internet stations. RuneScape is the most popular online RPG that is free to play, even though the enticements to subscribe grow as a player advances. Because of the continuous nature of an online RPG, it's very difficult to have a RuneScape event. However, it's not impossible to wring some competitive elements if you have a group start all new characters and make a pact about how much they can play each day.

RPG elements can often be found in action, adventure, or simulation games, and the already stat-heavy sports games have seen some RPG conventions creep in over the years.

3.1.4 First-Person Shooters

First-person shooters (FPS) take their name from the fact that you usually spend the entire game looking down the barrel of a gun, which you shoot a lot. Often nauseating or disorienting to first-time players, the goal is maximum immersion into the game world and the game body of your player. The setting and story of these games covers a relatively wide spectrum, encompassing everything from Nazis to aliens to zombies to zombie aliens or Nazi zombies and alien Nazis or sometimes alien zombie Nazis; despite this diversity, most FPS games look and play similarly. With a solid gameplay model established and a large, predominantly (but not exclusively) male fanbase, innovations in this genre are typically along the lines of crates that you can now push instead of just shooting up and walls that actually get holes in them if shot at enough, that sort of thing. You may have guessed by now that these aren't my cup of tea, but these ultracompetitive, inherently violent games are a surefire way to attract a large and passionate audience. Whether or not your library wants to go this route is for you to decide, but never doubt that it will draw a crowd.

Shooters are also very well suited to a tournament event: most support multiconsole LAN play and have built-in modes and settings that can make it easy to administer a tournament. The biggest problem with an FPS tournament at a library is that the best games in the genre are rated M. Even though your teenage audience may play the game all the time at home, you'd better get parental permission in writing before you allow off-label play at a tournament.

Shooters are often available for PCs and consoles, and installing an older, free, downloadable shooter on the PCs in an existing training center can be a quick way to get gaming events started. There are even some PC shooters, like Call of Duty, that allow you to turn off blood and guts to make the gameplay a little less gory.

FIRST-PERSON SHOOTERS	
Tournamentability	👾 👾 👾 👾 👾
Openplayability	👾 👾 👾 👾
Kids	👾
Teens	👾 👾 👾 👾 👾
Adults	👾 👾 👾 👾
Ratings E	👾
T	👾 👾 👾 👾
M	👾 👾 👾 👾 👾

SUBGENRE	DEFINING FRANCHISE
Occult Shooter	Doom/Quake
User-Modifiable Shooter	Unreal
Sci-Fi Shooter	Halo
Historical Shooter	Call of Duty
Realistic Shooter	Battlefront

3.1.5 Racing Games

Racing games are a staple of the industry and have a wide appeal. The combined challenge of the course and human opponents makes for intense matches, fevered rivalries between leaders, and plenty of opportunities for last-minute shake-ups and thrilling come-from-behind wins. The wide range of quality titles available provides opportunities to attract large audiences, and the ever-escalating skill level as you progress through a tournament series will make racing games seem fresh and irresistible long after the title can be found in the discount bin.

RACING GAMES	
Tournamentability	👾 👾 👾 👾 👾
Openplayability	👾 👾 👾
Kids	👾 👾 👾
Teens	👾 👾 👾 👾 👾
Adults	👾 👾 👾 👾
Ratings E	👾 👾 👾
T	👾 👾 👾 👾
M	👾

SUBGENRE	DEFINING FRANCHISE
Mascot Racer	Mario Kart
Crash Racer	Burnout/FlatOut
Obsessively Realistic Racer	Gran Turismo
Futuristic Hovering Racer	Wipeout/F-Zero
Arcade Racer	Daytona USA/Cruis'n USA

Racing games are extremely well suited to the tournament environment, with most titles featuring multiplayer modes and leaving no question about who won and who lost. A single title will also offer enough courses and modes to keep players coming back for more, and races are usually short enough to give all players several chances to play during an event. And unless you choose the edgier, "bonus points for pedestrians" types of titles, racing games can also sidestep much of the hand-wringing that other genres can encourage. See section 3.2.1 for more.

3.1.6 Fighting Games

Fighting games distill the competitive urge to its purest form: *must beat other guy*. Mastering a fighting game usually requires rising above "button mashing" and studying the often arcane button sequences required to execute a specific character's devastating special moves. This rewards the players for their dedication and drives them to seek out places to demonstrate their prowess, preferably in front of attractive members of the desired sex.

Fighting games are a huge draw, but you certainly can't say that they sidestep any hand-wringing about videogames producing bloodthirsty hellions, with the possible exception of the deep, cute, Pokémon-laden Super Smash Bros. (see section 3.2.2). However, the best titles in this genre are rated T, and it's easy to tell from the rating label what factors are present in a title. Be aware that the eighteen- to thirty-four-year-old-boy target market has left its mark on the entire genre; most titles will feature bulbous, gravity-defying breasts, and some titles will even allow you to adjust how much they jiggle. I'm not kidding.

Irrespective of the jiggle factor, fighting games are a great choice for a tournament. Short matches, clear victories, and varied character and level matchups make for lots of play time and intense competition for your players. No fighters really have a LAN mode, but you don't need it; each station can just be its own match. The more stations, the more play time for everyone, and

FIGHTING GAMES			
Tournamentability	👾 👾 👾 👾 👾		
Openplayability	👾 👾 👾 👾 👾		
Kids	👾		
Teens	👾 👾 👾 👾 👾		
Adults	👾 👾 👾		
Ratings E	👾		
T	👾 👾 👾 👾 👾		
M	👾 👾 👾		
SUBGENRE	**DEFINING FRANCHISE**		
Weapons Fighter	Soul Calibur		
Gory Fighter	Mortal Kombat		
Mascot Fighter	Super Smash Bros.		
Martial Arts Fighter	Tekken		
Wrestler	WCW v. NWO		

although the scorekeeping gets trickier, the setup scales easily. Fighting games are a huge draw, especially for teen boys, but be prepared to defend every configuration decision you make, as most players will seek to eliminate any elements that could result in them possibly losing to a player of lesser skill.

3.1.7 Sports Games

Sports games are top sellers on every console, and with many franchises providing incremental yearly updates with new rosters and a few new features, they're a very lucrative business. Electronic Arts owns most of this business and even negotiated a deal with the NFL that gives Madden exclusive rights to NFL teams, players, and stadiums. Naturally, sports games have a wide appeal to sports fans and provide increasingly realistic and detailed simulations of TV broadcasts of sporting events.

Because of complex control schemes, sports games are rarely pick-up-and-play, with the exception of arcade-style or mascot sports games that aim for accessibility and simple fun over realism. Matches can also often last thirty minutes or more, making it challenging to run a tournament for a crowd, even with several stations. In my experience, the fans of sports games can be hard to reach and more reluctant to come to the library, but every community is different, and you may find that sports games are a great place to start. They certainly sidestep most content concerns, and it's easy to tell who wins and who loses in each match. As in fighting games, your players will have a somewhat nebulous conception of what settings, plays, or teams are "cheap," so be prepared to hear complaints and attempt to identify the valid ones.

Also, because of the yearly update cycle of Electronic Arts'

SPORTS GAMES	
Tournamentability	☗ ☗ ☗
Openplayability	☗ ☗ ☗ ☗
Kids	☗ ☗
Teens	☗ ☗ ☗ ☗ ☗
Adults	☗ ☗ ☗ ☗
Ratings E	☗ ☗ ☗
T	☗ ☗ ☗ ☗ ☗
M	☗

SUBGENRE	DEFINING FRANCHISE
Football	Madden NFL
Basketball	NBA Live
Hockey	NHL
Baseball	MLB
Skateboarding	Tony Hawk
Snowboarding	SSX
Olympics	Most Olympic games stink
Golf	Links/Tiger Woods
Arcade Sports	NFL Blitz/NBA Jam
Mascot Sports	Mario Golf/ Mario Tennis/ Mario Baseball/ Mario Soccer/ Mario Basketball

line in particular, you may not get the same useful life out of a sports software purchase that you would typically get with a game from another genre. You can probably get away with doing last year's release, but offer a tournament on a sports game from two seasons ago and you're likely to turn off the very audience you're hoping to attract.

3.1.8 Simulations

The simulation genre is found most frequently on PCs, because the higher-resolution displays, greater power, larger storage, and presence of a mouse and keyboard better accommodate the complexity of a simulation. Some of the most popular simulations are ported to consoles, though usually with a reduced feature set.

The idea of a simulation, oddly enough, is to simulate a complex scenario and put the player at the helm. SimCity casts the player as an über-mayor, in control of zoning and public works but not development, having to chase the industrial, commercial, and residential needs of a community in pursuit of some sort of well-oiled utopia. At the other end, players of The Sims give instructions to residents of a household they create, telling them when to wake up, when to go to work, when to eat, and when to go to the bathroom. Sounds fun, right? That's the appeal of these games: having near-complete control over a virtual world, with scant goals other than to continually improve your situation.

As a result, it's very difficult to host simulation tournaments. Many simulations (with the notable exception of Civilization) have no multiplayer mode and no way to gauge completion, determine relative success, or even ensure equal opportunity. Matches often take a very long time to do right and aren't fair if truncated. Open simulation play can work if you have enough stations and can allow a single player to tie up a station for a few hours. You may be able to do simulation open play in an existing training center by installing some older, cheaper

SIMULATIONS	
Tournamentability	🕹 🕹
Openplayability	🕹 🕹 🕹
Kids	🕹 🕹
Teens	🕹 🕹 🕹 🕹 🕹
Adults	🕹 🕹 🕹 🕹
Ratings E	👾 👾 👾
T	👾 👾 👾 👾 👾
M	👾 👾 👾
SUBGENRE	**DEFINING FRANCHISE**
Mayor Sim	SimCity
Emperor Sim	Civilization
Household Sim	The Sims
Flight Sim	Flight Simulator
Business Sim	Tycoon
Virtual Pet	Dogz/Nintendogs/ Black and White

simulations to get the ball rolling. Also, simulations are relatively cerebral (especially Civilization and the Tycoon series), and they can allow you to demonstrate the learning potential of gaming events to those who would otherwise be difficult to convince.

3.1.9 Strategy

While strategy games all involve elements of simulation, and usually some adventure and role playing as well, the focus is on individual battles, moving units around, and gaining control of precious resources. Almost all strategy games have multiplayer modes and make for challenging, complex tournaments. Most popular are those in the real-time strategy (RTS) subgenre, where the play is not broken up into artificial turns or phases, requiring players to reconnoiter, plan, supply, and issue orders to units while gameplay is in progress. Warcraft and StarCraft are probably the most popular games in this genre, even years after their release. StarCraft tournaments are actually so big in game-crazy South Korea that matches are televised nationally to audiences of millions.

Like simulation games, most strategy games got their start on the PC, with the most popular titles finding their way to consoles. However, in recent years, a few high-quality strategy franchises for consoles have emerged, most notably the outstanding Advance Wars series for Game Boy Advance and DS and the brilliant, underappreciated Pikmin series for GameCube.

With the right settings, matches can be kept to a controllable length, but those settings decisions should only be made with the input of an expert player to avoid a faux pas. However, almost all strategy games have a war theme of varying degrees of realism, so if you're concerned about backlash, this may not be a good place to start. And although I won't hazard a guess as to why, this game genre may well be the least popular with females.

STRATEGY		
Tournamentability	👾 👾 👾	
Openplayability	👾 👾 👾 👾	
Kids	👾 👾	
Teens	👾 👾 👾 👾	
Adults	👾 👾 👾 👾 👾	
Ratings **E**	👾	
T	👾 👾 👾 👾	
M	👾 👾 👾	
SUBGENRE	**DEFINING FRANCHISE**	
Real-Time Strategy	Command and Conquer/ Warcraft/ StarCraft	
Space Fleet Commander	Homeworld	
Turn-Based Strategy	Fire Emblem/ Romance of the Three Kingdoms	
RPG Strategy	Final Fantasy Tactics/Tactics Ogre	
Handheld Strategy	Advance Wars	
Console Strategy	Pikmin	

3.1.10 Oddball Games

There is a class of videogames, especially those from our friends in Japan, that are so strange and iconoclastic that their weirdness is a more dominant characteristic than any particular gameplay mechanic. That's a good thing: weird games shake things up and keep players guessing. In addition, many mainstream gamers may not own or may never have played some of the more obscure titles, giving you an opportunity to expose your players to some quality titles they might not otherwise have seen, just like we try to do with our other collections!

ODDBALL GAMES	
Tournamentability	▦ ▦ ▦ ▦
Openplayability	▦ ▦ ▦ ▦ ▦
Kids	▦ ▦ ▦ ▦
Teens	▦ ▦ ▦ ▦ ▦
Adults	▦ ▦ ▦
Ratings E	▦ ▦ ▦ ▦
T	▦ ▦ ▦ ▦
M	▦

SUBGENRE	DEFINING FRANCHISE
Weird Rhythm	PaRappa the Rappa
Microgames	WarioWare
Party Board Game	Mario Party
Sticky Rolling Thing	Katamari Damacy

You don't want to overuse oddball titles in an entire season and let the novelty wear off, but as stand-alone events or at an open play, they rarely fail to please and get the whole room laughing. These games usually have multiplayer capabilities, especially in the party games that are intended to be played by as many people as possible, and will often have tournament modes built in.

These games will usually be very short on realistic violence and hypersexualized characters, but some titles, especially those from Japan, may have a frankness toward bodily functions that is a little too frank for more reserved U.S. tastes. For example, there's a song in the original PaRappa the Rappa, an early rhythm game, that has our hero desperate to get to the gas station bathroom after overeating at a picnic. I don't think I need to get into what happens if you fail the level. WarioWare also features several microgames (very short minigames) that involve trying to get a finger placed perfectly up a moving nostril and others that feature, um, other body parts. Trust me, it's really fun.

3.1.11 Rhythm, Music, and Physical Games

If you could only pick one type of game to play at your library, pick one of these (see section 3.2.3). Rhythm games have a wide appeal, are great for beginners, encourage intense cooperation and competition, and have the added bonus of getting players up and moving around. Basically, each game has its own way of showing you what moves or buttons or drum hits or strums you're supposed to do and when, usually involving a scrolling display, and the goal is to perform the specified actions as accurately as possible for the highest score. It can get quite intense at the higher levels, making for exciting, highly competitive matches.

Predominantly produced for consoles with a few PC-based clones (most notably the amazing open-source DDR clone, StepMania), these games will often require the use of a unique controller, like a

RHYTHM, MUSIC, AND PHYSICAL GAMES	
Tournamentability	🎮 🎮 🎮 🎮 🎮
Openplayability	🎮 🎮 🎮 🎮 🎮
Kids	🎮 🎮 🎮
Teens	🎮 🎮 🎮 🎮 🎮
Adults	🎮 🎮 🎮 🎮
Ratings E	🎮 🎮 🎮 🎮
T	🎮 🎮 🎮 🎮
M	🎮
Dance Dance Revolution	Guitar Hero
Beatmania	Wii Sports
Donkey Konga	Karaoke Revolution

dance mat, a set of bongos, or a miniature guitar. While there is a lot of room to improve the skills required to play these games, most people can pick up and play an easy level once someone shows them what to do. It's certainly more intuitive than thumb twiddling, although it is pretty hard to succeed at a rhythm game if one has no sense of rhythm. They'll still have fun, though.

The best aspect of rhythm games is that because most support multi-player matches with each player at their own difficulty level, they allow for better intergenerational gaming opportunities than any other genre. It's easy to construct tournaments that give advantage or dedicated prizes to parent-child teams or the like and get players of wide age ranges involved together.

While there is very little to complain about in the central gameplay of these titles, many are rated T simply for the suggestive lyrics of the pop songs they include and rarely present a problem. DDR sometimes shows the music video for the selected song, which can be a little over the line for a young audience, so watch out for that and turn off the videos if you're worried.

3.1.12 Retro Games

While videogames are a fast-moving business and gamers are a bunch of neophiliacs, no gamer can deny the simple appeal and pure gameplay of "retro" videogames, usually meaning those that were released before 1990. Younger teens and kids may well have never played these games before, although popular web games retread some of the best old gameplay mechanics over and over again, so the concepts will often be familiar.

You don't necessarily need to drag the Atari out of the basement to be able to play old games; all modern consoles have compilations of classic games available that allow the original software to be played using modern hardware and controllers. Both Wii and Xbox 360 have growing lists of classic games available for low-cost download. Wii even has a special retro controller just for playing older games.

That said, if you have a working Atari, schlep it out and show those whippersnappers what the dark ages were like. Retro games are great for short, informal tournaments, and players love to mess around with retro compilations at an open play. You can have a tournament based on a single game or set of games or have an ongoing high-score contest for Pac-Man, Defender, or other single-player games. Retro tournaments also have a wide appeal, from the nostalgic parents to the curious elementary schoolers who marvel at the blocky worlds we were somehow satisfied with.

Retro games are inexpensive and simple to configure, and most offer that forgotten metric called "score" that can make it very easy to run large tournaments where each player plays several different games going for the highest total score. Add separate brackets for teenage, youth, and adult players, and you've got a fun multigenerational event that will be warmly received by gamers of all ages in your community.

RETRO GAMES	
Tournamentability	👾👾👾👾👾
Openplayability	👾👾👾👾
Kids	👾👾👾👾
Teens	👾👾👾👾
Adults	👾👾👾👾👾
Ratings　　E	👾👾👾👾
T	👾👾👾
M	👾
Pac-Man	Rampage
Marble Madness	Joust
Rampart	Pong

3.2 Recommended Games for Tournaments, and an Unapologetic Fanboy's Disclaimer

OK, before I start telling you which specific software I think is the best for library tournaments, and just in case you haven't figured it out already, you need to know that I am one of those fanboys whose opinions I recommend taking with a grain of salt. Yes, I am a Nintendo fanboy, with the Triforce tattoo to show for it. I think that Nintendo consistently turns out the most finely polished, widely engaging, and innovative software. I thrive on the bright, clean look of classic Nintendo-developed games.

Also, first-person shooters, or other highly violent games, are just not my thing, so I don't pursue those options with the same zeal that I would throw at an event featuring a mushroom-eating Italian plumber. As you read through my recommendations, you may wish to consider my bias as I continually advocate lighter Nintendo titles over their darker competitors. But I stand firm on the statement that Nintendo continues to eventually deliver the most consistently deep and high-quality gameplay from their admittedly heavily stylized titles; and while you are entitled to disagree with me, you would be wrong. OK, onward!

3.2.1 Mario Kart and Other Racing Games

As mentioned in section 3.1.5, racing games, due to their quick, high-capacity matches, easily determined victories, and wide appeal, are a great place for a library to start a gaming program. While single racing events are always highly competitive, the real competition comes over a series of events as players improve and dominant players are crowned and subsequently dethroned. Your audience will continue to develop their skills by playing each other, and the overall level of play will visibly increase. This rising tide of skill also helps keep older racing games fresh and dynamic, as the challenge of unfamiliar courses fades against the challenge posed by ever-faster opponents.

Mario Kart is, in my humble and entirely biased opinion, simply the finest racing franchise yet developed. Mario Kart remains unequaled in delivering tight, challenging racing without getting frustrating or requiring undue precision. Mario Kart games are more finely tuned and balanced than any of their mascot racer genre competitors and rival the depth of much more serious titles while possessing a far broader appeal.

While kart racing isn't for everyone, it is easy to pick up due to a relatively simple control scheme, and it offers a rewarding play experience to kids, teens, and adults. Not all titles play so well at all levels, although nongamer adults may struggle to process what's happening on the screen. Mario Kart is also notable for having fairly rigid multiplayer settings: the random and balancing elements can't be turned off. This may sound like a negative, but the fact is that there won't be any arguments about whether items are unfair in a Mario Kart race. Mario Kart Double Dash in LAN mode simply chooses randomly what characters and karts each player gets to drive, completely sidestepping a time-consuming and contentious part of starting a race. Players at the back of the pack are more likely to get powerful items to help them catch up. Few games are so well tuned to deliver fast, competitive races where it's still possible to recover from a mistake, but it can happen in Mario Kart, if you're lucky.

Mario Kart Double Dash for GameCube has held up very well and will be playable on the Wii, although the Wii will unfortunately not support Double Dash's LAN mode. There will certainly be a new Mario Kart game for Wii, but it might not be released until 2008 or even later. Until then, Mario Kart Double Dash remains an excellent choice for tournaments and open play at a library, with a wide age appeal and a deep, rewarding skill curve.

Mario Kart also offers battle modes (and many other racers do too) that allow you to have several different types of events within the same game. During the first season, AADL offered both single-player and team race and battle events, wringing a four-event tournament out of a single game and setup.

If you're not going the Nintendo route (for shame!), you're better off with a more serious racer, like Project Gotham Racing for the Xbox 360 or one from the Burnout series, as most Mario Kart clones don't deliver the same level of play. In any case, a racing game should be a staple of your kit or collection. They make for straightforward, competitive tournaments and have wide appeal for existing gamers, even if they're not necessarily the friendliest to beginners.

Always try to offer qualification heats in a racing tournament to avoid players getting eliminated in the first ten minutes of a three-hour event. See section 7.3 for more about heats, but I always try to offer at least three qualification races for each player before taking the top thirty-two players to single-elimination rounds.

3.2.2 Super Smash Bros. Melee and Other Fighting Games

Competition in a social setting, especially when teenagers are involved, is not just about victory; it's about *superiority.* No one will thank luck for a win (though they'll always blame it for a loss), and fighting games provide a venue in which a powerful display of superiority over your opponents can provide unassailable proof of your incontestable awesomeness. That's what keeps gamers coming back. The draw of fighting games, while not exactly broad, is very powerful, and whatever fighting games you provide will likely be the most popular titles at an open play and your most heavily attended tournaments.

As you've probably guessed, however, you'll need to make this choice carefully to provide a satisfying play experience to your gamers without awakening the ire of the nongaming concerned citizens, or even worse the nongaming journalists, of your community. Most fighting games (and all the top sellers) are rated T, so you don't really need to worry about highly inappropriate content for a teenage audience; however, that doesn't guarantee that a board member's neighbor won't be shocked, *shocked* to see such acts of (half-)naked aggression encouraged at the public library. Even relatively tame and not-so-prurient titles like Soul Calibur or Tekken may be too much for your community or governing body.

If that's the case, or you just want to avoid stepping in that situation altogether, Super Smash Bros. Melee for GameCube (and its Wii sequel, Super Smash Bros. Brawl) may be just the title for you. Super Smash Bros. Melee is the top-selling GameCube title, featuring two- to four-player hand-to-hand battles between characters from Nintendo's stable of licenses, including Mario, Donkey Kong, Kirby, Pokémon, Star Fox, Zelda, and many others. These are cartoon characters hitting each other. No blood, no dismemberment, and not even any knockouts; you lose a life when you're knocked so far off the stage by an opponent's attack that you can't get back on. While it's a fighting game that is highly unlikely to arouse any nongamer ire—unless you let the young kids play it—it's also a phenomenally deep game with sophisticated controls and a tight balance between characters and their abilities.

To give you an idea of how highly respected the Super Smash Bros. Melee play mechanic is, there's an organization called Major League Gaming (MLG) that is working to expand and sanction gaming tournaments around the world and raise the profile of videogame competitions. MLG tournaments in 2005 featured just two games: Halo 2 and Super Smash Bros. Melee. Super Smash tournaments are serious business and respected by serious players around the world, despite the game's cartoonish, mild appearance.

Along with such seriousness come a lot of expectations from your audience about what is and isn't fair within the possibilities of configuring a match. There are even official fan regulations to which you may wish to adhere, governing allowed stages, round formats, and even the sequence by which the players choose their characters.

With fighting games, and Super Smash is no exception, it's important to have a memory card that includes a game save for the title, with everything (stages, players, even costumes) unlocked. If you don't have this before your first tournament, odds are one of the players will bring one. Just be ready to have them copy it onto your memory card for you.

Like racing games, fighting games are great for tournaments because of the intense competition, short matches (depending on your settings), and high capacity. Unlike racing games, however, few fighting games support a multiconsole LAN mode. Instead, you'll run several concurrent matches on the stations you have available. Again, I always like to provide a few qualification matches in a fighting game, building up scores, before anyone is eliminated.

Fighting games tend to have a stronger but narrower appeal than racing or rhythm games, attracting mostly teenage or college boys and almost no girls. Although it doesn't have as much crossover potential, fighting games will pull in a big crowd once word spreads and can be a great way to jump-start events for the sizable hard-core teenage gamer crowd.

If Super Smash isn't your cup of tea, Soul Calibur is the best alternative: a historical weapons fighter with detailed characters and stages, no gore or fatalities, and only mildly skimpy outfits (with a few cringeworthy exceptions). Next would be Tekken, still very popular but with a more arcane play mechanic. At any rate, you should have a fighting game in your kit or collection, and you should try to plan a fighting tournament as part of your inaugural season (see section 4.2).

3.2.3 Dance Dance Revolution and Other Rhythm Games

If you play just one game at your library, it should be Dance Dance Revolution (DDR). Unlike most other videogames that have no choice but to suffer, much maligned and misunderstood, on the cover of *USA Today,* DDR is actually riding a positive publicity wave thanks to its ability to get those listless, desultory teens up off the couch and sweating to the point where they actually take a shower of their own accord (if you're lucky).

DDR has many different versions with different sets of songs, but the core gameplay is the same: you stand on a pad with up, down, left, and right arrows at your feet. Arrows move up the screen in time to the music; when an arrow reaches the top of the screen, you step on that arrow. You're then scored based on your accuracy. It's a very simple idea that players of all ages and skill levels can quickly grasp and enjoy; but the arrows can fly fast and furious at higher levels, posing a significant physical challenge that requires dedication and practice to overcome.

Which brings us to one of the best features of the DDR series: two players can play at once, each getting their own set of arrows at their chosen skill level, which allows beginners to play alongside more experienced players without having to match their skill. This enables parent-child events, special over-thirty brackets at otherwise teen-dominated tournaments, and other opportunities that most games can't match.

For each arrow that moves up the screen, the game keeps track of how accurately the player stepped on the right arrow, assigning each step a success rating from marvelous, perfect, and great to good, boo, or even miss. At the end of each match, the screen displays a table of all the ratings that each player has achieved, giving you several scoring options based on player feedback (I simply record the number of perfects).

One of the best things about starting a DDR event is that you can do a large tournament with only one station. I routinely do tournaments for about one hundred DDR players of all ages with only one PlayStation 2, two dance pads, a projector, and an amplifier. I take registration in pairs, then go through the list twice so that each player gets two dances spaced apart. I then total up their perfects from their two dances and sort by the total score, taking the top sixteen players on to head-to-head elimination.

DDR has a wide appeal and is very popular with girls. You may find that you need to have separate teen and kid/adult tournaments to keep your teenage audience from overwhelming an event that was intended to be for all ages. Of course, it's nice to have this kind of problem. Because DDR is so simple to set up, run, and score, it's a great way for a library to get into tournaments and start forging a new relationship with the gamers in the community.

In addition to DDR, you may wish to explore tournaments and open play for other great rhythm games out there such as Donkey Konga, DDR Mario Mix for GameCube, which is very accessible to younger kids, Taiko Drum Master, the amazing Guitar Hero for PlayStation 2, or even Karaoke Revolution for Xbox, PlayStation 2, or GameCube. Again, all can be done with fewer stations and less play time than other games, especially if you have other stuff scattered about the room for people to do while they're waiting for their next turn (maybe some of your manga collection or gaming magazines). Just leave the hard covers on the shelf.

3.2.4 The Sports Conundrum

Sports games are a cornerstone of the game market and are highly popular with what you might call mainstream (as opposed to hard-core) gamers. Just like in fighting or racing games, these players take pride in their skill and relish the opportunity to lord it over an inferior player. However, in my experience, sports games do not come even close to delivering the numbers to which I've become accustomed at a Super Smash or DDR tournament. Every community is different, and Madden or NBA Live may be the top requests of your after-school crowd, but they may not be as well suited or as essential for larger tournaments as a fighting, racing, or rhythm game could be. Also, as mentioned in section 3.1.7, the relatively large amount of time required for a fair sports match can be prohibitive, and sports games can have an even narrower appeal than fighting games.

One way to make the most of a sports game audience without bumping up against time limits too much is to offer an open play season that spans a few events. You can prepare a schedule of matches for each player, have a miniseason over a few days, and then move on to the playoffs and give prizes to the champions. This works especially well if you've got a place to leave the equipment set up and have a group of kids who come every day after school. It may even be a constructive way to entertain groups that could otherwise be disruptive.

Sports games also generally work well in open play situations as long as you set some limits on match length to keep the stations turning over if needed. You could even split the difference and encourage the players to organize their own tournament or season during an open play and see where they take it.

Another good aspect of sports games is that they again sidestep many content concerns. Most sports games are seeking to emulate a television broadcast as closely as possible, staying well within the bounds of what most people would consider appropriate for all ages. Choosing a sports game for your kit or collection depends on your community more than other genres, due to different cultural and regional sports preferences: perhaps college football is bigger in your community than the NFL, or maybe basketball or hockey is the big thing. You might buy one of each and see what gets the biggest crowd at an open play. Just keep in mind that sports games will often have a shorter life span than games in other genres due to the season-specific rosters and yearly upgrades.

3.2.5 PC Games and LAN Parties

As you've surely noticed, most of this book has been about console games. There's a whole other side to gaming, the PC side. While many great titles show up on both PCs and consoles, the PC gaming world is very different from the console gaming world, with more facets, more technical challenges, and more issues involved in getting an event off the ground.

First, I'll make a distinction between web/online games, which are played in or launched from a web browser, and installable games, which are distributed on a CD or downloaded and are a separate program that must be installed on a PC before use. Web games are probably in your library already—chess, Scrabble, poker, Bejeweled, RuneScape, hearts, euchre. Most of these games have their social elements built in, and an event can add little to them. However, RuneScape events can make a solution out of a problem, and creative event planning can turn almost any web game into an event if you've got scores to compare and a set of PCs to use.

Installable games offer some truly great event options. Almost all major PC games offer LAN play, and although it can be far more challenging to get working than console LANs, some older titles are even available for free. You may be able to install an old copy of Call of Duty in your older training center and have sixteen stations ready to play on demand. There are also more options for your players to be creative, as PC games tend to be highly modifiable. You may have players in your community who like to play, but what they really want is to play human opponents on a map that they designed in their free time.

I wouldn't recommend getting into computer games if you don't already have a set of PCs that could be pressed into service. As discussed in section 3.3.5, trying to have even a single PC that can keep up with software releases can be daunting and expensive. However, if you have a facility that would be great for a tournament but just happens to be full of computers, there are definitely some options you should explore. One particularly interesting title is BZFlag, an open-source tank FPS that runs well on older hardware and allows for fast, furious, no-frills mayhem. You can even run your own BZFlag server and allow your PC-owning patrons to play from home.

Nowadays large, even huge, PC game tournaments are a fixture of the geek world, and they're usually of the BYOC (bring your own computer) sort. These LAN parties provide tables, power, network cables, and hubs; the players schlep in their own computers and monitors, hook them all up to the network, and frag all day. This may already be happening somewhere in your community, and they may even be paying for space to hold this event. Finding those groups and offering them space for a LAN party can be a quick way to get gaming into the library with very little expense or expertise required.

3.2.6 Retro, Oddball, and Other Draws

With a few cornerstones of the software landscape all picked out, you've got to throw in a few wildcards and expose your players to some titles they may not have played before, or maybe show them new ways to play the games they play all the time.

Every game kit or collection should have a few retro compilations as mentioned in section 3.1.12. The Namco Museum and Midway Arcade Treasures series are particularly good titles, as well as Taito Legends for PlayStation 2. Old games will not only satisfy curious players at open play events, but they also provide the possibility of retro tournaments that are nostalgic for us old fogies and a charming novelty to the whippersnappers. These titles are usually inexpensive and can entertain for hours. It's also nice for these young'uns to respect their elders by understanding the cripplingly low resolution of digital life in the early 1980s.

Along with retro compilations, you should consider a weird title or two to keep things interesting. Katamari Damacy is always a good choice, although it's almost not even weird anymore. There are also some seriously strange rhythm games for PlayStation 2 that use the regular controller, like PaRappa the Rappa 2 or Gitaroo Man that every gamer should try at least once. But the king of weird is unquestionably WarioWare for GameCube, as mentioned in section 3.1.10. WarioWare is great for open play poking around, but it really shines as a simple, yet inexplicable tournament game for a very strange tournament. Along those lines, you should consider the purchase of a party game. Mario Party is the definitive franchise, but several of its imitators (that usually have "party" in the title) are good for open play fun or short tournaments.

Finally, in the play-in-a-new-way department, there is an opportunity for the library to get in on the still-burgeoning Pokémon craze by holding Pokémon tournaments where players bring in their own Pokémon and their own Game Boys. A few different GameCube titles, as well as Pokémon Battle Revolution for Wii, will allow players to have their Pokémon fight each other on the big screen, with far better graphics, environments, and effects than the Game Boy is capable of. Few of even the most hardcore Pokéfans will ever have tried this, so just pulling together a copy of Pokémon XD for GameCube and two GameCube–Game Boy cables can deliver a play experience that they've never had before. With only one station again, it's a quick setup, and to the older elementary crowd, it's just Meowth's pajamas.

So, when you're making the list of software that you'd like to offer at open plays or tournaments, keep these considerations in mind and select a wide range of titles to maximize your service's appeal, and then select the console (or consoles) that will let you play the most of your chosen titles.

3.3 Choosing Your Hardware, or Why You Should Have Chosen Your Software First

Once you know which available or upcoming software you want to offer at your library (or if you've decided that I'm full of it and you're going to buy the console that your teenage son says you should buy and worry about software later), you're ready to make a console decision. If you've scared up enough funding to make an initial investment, you'll want to make the most of your money. Here's what you need to know to help avoid costly surprises.

3.3.1 Things to Consider, or The Dawning of Console War VII

Hopefully you know by now what software you want and the best console to run the software. However, many of the most popular titles are available for more than one console with some minor differences, so it can still be a puzzle to decide which console will best meet your needs, especially surrounded by the opening sorties of the next console war.

The game console business is an iterative beast, and most historians agree that the current (as of early 2007) slate of consoles represents the seventh generation of directly competing hardware offerings. The first generation included the home version of Pong, released in 1975, and each generation has lasted about five years. Because many homes still only purchase one console for each generation (although two-console homes are on the rise), competition for market share is intense, and each offering is aggressively marketed—hence, the "war" part.

In console war VII, we have offerings from three titans of industry— Nintendo's Wii, Sony's PlayStation 3, and Microsoft's Xbox 360—firing salvos of technology and ad buys furiously as they jockey for market share, dominance, and the resultant piles of money. Together, these three companies will likely sell a total of 150 million game consoles over the next several years, and the way that pie is sliced will determine who makes a killing and who takes a bath.

Bear in mind that you don't only have to consider the next generation's consoles at this point. Software takes time to mature, and the hot new consoles still have very young software libraries. Don't exclude the venerable Sony PlayStation 2 or the Nintendo GameCube, especially if funds are tight. There's certainly a downside to using the older technology with the hard-core crowd; it's frankly what they would expect of a fuddy-duddy joint like the library. However, you will get plenty of people coming to play these slightly older games, and it's another good way to jump-start a service for less.

The backward compatibility (the ability to play old games on a new system) is something you should keep in mind if you are going for a new console; having access to a large back catalog of established titles can be a big plus for your new console. The PlayStation 3 is compatible with most PlayStation or PlayStation 2 games, although it will not currently support PlayStation 2 controllers or other controller-port peripherals (like dance pads). Nintendo Wii supports all Nintendo GameCube titles, controllers, and memory cards, but not Mario Kart's LAN mode. An Xbox 360 with a hard drive will support many of the Xbox's most popular titles, but compatibility is implemented for each game specifically, and game-specific updates need to be downloaded over the Internet.

If you are able to buy more than one console, think about the size, scale, and type of events you're likely to produce. It may be tempting to punt on the purchase decision and buy one or two of each kind, and that will work well if you're going to stick with open plays only. If you're going to do tournaments, however, and you have the room for them to grow into large events, it's going to be a challenge to get good use out of several different consoles, even if you have the same game for each. The versions will have small differences that will make the tournament unfair. For tournaments, you want to have as many identical stations as you can, so you may wish to make a decision and stick with it.

Be sure to consider the operating costs of each console as you're making your choice. In addition to the purchase price, look at the costs of peripherals, extra controllers, and especially the games. The cost of developing top-tier games keeps increasing, and the publishers are looking to pass as much of that cost on to consumers as they can get away with.

It is also worth considering the cachet factor. Especially here at the dawn of a new generation, you can get an audience just by offering them some quality time with a console they haven't had much chance to play yet and its highly appealing software. If you can pull together hardware and software to deliver experiences that they can't get so easily at home, you've added a significant draw to your service.

Finally, before you freak out completely, remember that you don't need to buy anything to get your gaming service off the ground. See section 6.7 for ideas on ways to start your service without making major purchases. However, if you get the funding and are planning on buying equipment, here's some guidance on how to make that decision.

3.3.2   Microsoft and Its Xboxen

Microsoft entered the console business in 2001 with the release of the Xbox, determined to capture the hearts, minds, and wallets of the burgeoning hard-core gamer market. Armed with the exclusive Halo franchise, Xbox sold extremely well to teens and young men, with relatively few titles appealing to casual or female gamers (maybe they should have called it the XYbox). Even though the Xbox sold 24 million units and developed a powerful brand following among its target demographic, Microsoft has not yet made a dime on the endeavor. When it came time for a successor for the Xbox, Microsoft took advantage of incremental upgrades in the underlying technology to get a new console out the door quickly, and the Xbox 360 had a full year head start on the PlayStation 3 and the Wii. Note that it's not called the Xbox 2; who would buy an Xbox 2 when they could have a PlayStation 3?

At any rate, the Xbox has a dedicated following, and in the standard-setting shooter, Halo, a bona fide smash hit franchise. Bill Gates once said that they would launch Halo 3 on the same day that the PlayStation 3 launched, just to be rude, although that didn't really happen. The Xbox 360 has sold about 11 million units as of this writing with its combination of slick looks and graphics, a solid but predictable software library with appeal to hard-core gamers, and the outstanding Xbox Live online subscription service, which offers online play, matchmaking, social tools, and for-fee downloadable games from the Xbox Live Arcade (XBLA).

Because of broad LAN play support, the Xbox 360 offers many titles that would be well suited to tournaments or open plays, including most prominent racing and FPS franchises. The games are generally polished and look sharp, especially on high-end televisions. The Xbox 360 is a good choice if your goal is to attract hard-core gamers, as the brand carries significant cachet and predominantly features the darker, edgier titles that teenage boys love. However, if you're looking to branch out to younger, older, or more casual gamers, the retail software available for the Xbox 360 has little to offer. The exceptions are the titles available on XBLA; downloadable over the Internet for a small fee and stored on the Xbox's hard drive, many XBLA games are more casual titles, including lots of retro games. One of the most popular games on XBLA is actually good old Uno. The costs to develop and distribute a game for XBLA are very low compared to a retail title, so in many cases that's where the Xbox's innovative titles are. If you are really looking to attract the dedicated hard-core gamers, a roomful of Xbox 360s is a good way to do it, but you may ultimately find that the units aren't as flexible as they would need to be to reach other gaming audiences.

3.3.3   Sony's PlayStation 1, 2, 3, and Beyond

The original PlayStation grew out of a failed partnership between Nintendo and Sony to produce a CD drive for the Super Nintendo. The PlayStation and the PlayStation 2 each went on to sell over 100 million units worldwide, with the PlayStation hitting over 30 percent household penetration in the United States at its peak. The power of that installed base turned PlayStation into a household name, guaranteed lots of software in the market, and built a powerful following for Sony.

Sony has bet the farm on the PlayStation 3, a mammoth, superpowerful console that offers about the same amount of raw, theoretical processing power as Intel's ASCII Option Red supercomputer offered Sandia National Laboratories. To put this in perspective, the device you're going to put under your TV in the living room in 2007 is theoretically more powerful than a device that only ten years ago required 106 cabinets and 2,500 square feet at a cost of $50 million! That's an insane amount of processing power, which is why Sony thinks you'll be happy to pay $600 for it.

Actually, it's not just the power of the PlayStation 3 that makes it expensive; Sony is also using the brand power of the PlayStation 3 to push their new high-definition movie format, called Blu-Ray. PlayStation 3 games will come on Blu-Ray discs, and you'll be able to watch Blu-Ray movies in HD resolution on your new (hopefully Sony brand) HDTV. Sony has had success with this strategy before: the fact that the PlayStation 2 could play DVD movies was a strong selling point when many households did not yet have DVD players. On the other hand, Sony has not won many of the format wars it has engaged in (seen any Betamax tapes or minidiscs lately?).

However, that Blu-Ray drive is an expensive component, and by some estimates Sony could be losing as much as $200 or more on every Play-Station 3 they sell, although production costs will drop rapidly as sales take off. Regardless, this is a very powerful device that will deliver some sophisticated and realistic visual experiences.

Again, with their price point and built-in capabilities, Sony is going for the lucrative hard-core gamer market and fully engaging in an arms race with Microsoft to see whose box can push the most pixels per second. Sony's PlayStation 3 controller, although it has the same tried-and-true shape as the PlayStation 1 and PlayStation 2 controllers, is sensitive to rotation along all three axes, allowing for more immersive, motion-based gaming.

The current $600 price point alone is probably enough to disqualify the PlayStation 3 from a library purchase; it's hard to justify when you can get twice as many of another console. However, there are a few early titles for PlayStation 3 that would make good tournament games, such as Ridge Racer or the PlayStation 3 versions of Madden or NBA Live. Also, with the high price point, getting just one may be enough to draw in the gamer crowds; many people won't have one at home and will come just for a chance to play and see what all the fuss is about. It's also nice for a public library to be on the upswing of an adoption curve for a change; it would really impress the gamers in your community to find a roomful of PlayStation 3s, especially if they're accompanied by nice TVs.

The strength of the PlayStation brand, especially among more main-stream gamers, is sure to make the console a major force in the next generation. However, the hard-core audience has so far rebelled at the price point and unnecessarily fancy drive, making for an unlikely schism that could produce unexpected results. As of this writing, it's looking like that's exactly what's happening: while the PlayStation 3 launched with extremely short supplies, eBay prices quickly crashed, and the subsequent widespread retail availability (while people are still lining up for a chance to buy a Wii) is a dangerous indication of an indifferent "meh" from con-sumers. Demand will likely pick up as Christmas 2007 inches closer, but right now it looks like the PlayStation 3 may be a big problem for Sony.

3.3.4   Nintendo and the Plumber of the Future

If you happened to skip section 3.2, go back and read it now, then proceed. OK? OK. Nintendo single-handedly rebuilt the game business after Atari and E.T. the videogame killed it in the early 1980s, and for my generation, Nintendo is still synonymous with videogames and fun. Nintendo survived the end of their bitter rivalry with Sega only to see Sony's PlayStation rise to successes that Nintendo had never been able to achieve in terms of units sold. The GameCube, much maligned by Sony and Microsoft fanboys but with some of the best titles of its generation, has sold 21 million units worldwide, close behind the Xbox but a distant third to Sony's 100 million PlayStation 2s. This is often used as evidence that Nintendo lost the sixth generation; however, unlike Microsoft, Nintendo has made a profit throughout, including many quarters when both Sony and Microsoft were posting big losses.

So, as the seventh generation dawned, and it became increasingly clear that Microsoft and Sony were engaging in a no-holds-barred fight for technical supremacy, with gameplay quality a footnote and non-hard-core gamers hardly a consideration, Nintendo decided to opt out of the arms race and take a different tack. Starting with the bizarre, easily ridiculed name, Nintendo's Wii is positioned so differently from its competitors that it almost seems to be creating a new and different console market than the one that the Xbox 360 and the PlayStation 3 are squabbling over.

Starting with its modest, but not insignificant, performance increase, its miniscule proportions, and its low power consumption, the Wii takes the position that graphics are already mostly good enough and what really needs advancement is the gameplay. Of course, this is great fodder for Microsoft and Sony fanboys, who call the Wii a mildly souped-up GameCube. Interestingly, this idea is very appealing to cost-conscious game developers already familiar with GameCube development, who see the Wii as a way to develop new games without having to start from scratch.

The big news about the Wii, however, is its breakthrough new game controller. Shaped like a television remote and with far fewer buttons than its competitors, it's sensitive not only to rotation but also to position, allowing it to be used as a 3-D pointing device you can twist, turn, and flip. This makes for breakthrough gameplay opportunities with a new level of physical involvement for previously thumb-waggling players; use the "Wiimote" to hack and slash a sword, reel in a fish, suture an incision, or flip a wokful of food. To play racing games, you can turn the Wiimote sideways, like an older Nintendo controller, and turn it like a steering wheel, allowing for far more intuitive interaction than the relatively fine motor control required to steer with a thumbstick. To play tennis, you just hold it like a racket and swing.

To further depart from its competition, Wii features a channel-style interface, including weather and news channels, and a tool to create little on-screen caricatures of yourself that then appear as your avatar in supported games. You can even move your avatar (called a Mii, of course) onto your Wiimote and take it to a friend's house or send it to your Wii friends over the Internet.

Wii is poised to ride the growth of the burgeoning casual gamer market while still appealing to the hard core; its intuitive new control options offer greater accessibility to new gamers while offering something fresh to the veterans. It's well positioned in the market, with a launch price of $250, which includes a game (Wii Sports, with bowling, tennis, baseball, golf, and boxing) and compares favorably to the PlayStation 3 and even the Xbox.

Of course, that price point makes it very appealing to libraries, especially when you add in its backward compatibility and four GameCube controller ports that allow you to play all the great GameCube games I keep yammering about. In addition, Nintendo will be offering much of their (and even their long since vanquished competitors') back catalog of games available as for-fee downloads, bringing back some of the best games of the past twenty years.

Wii was the big story of Christmas 2006. People were camping out for every shipment like it was launch day, and this round of the battle of the buzz unquestionably went to Nintendo. You hear more nongamers talking about the Wii than have ever talked about videogames before. Anyone who tries Wii Sports is immediately hooked, and anyone can play it, especially people who have never played videogames before. Conan O'Brien had Serena Williams on his late-night show, and he made her play Wii Sports tennis against him (he won). The Wii has moved so quickly into the mainstream, and demand remains so strong well after the holiday season, that it looks like Nintendo may be on its way back to the top of the market.

In my entirely biased fanboy opinion, I think that Wii is the best option for libraries going forward. Its fun, innovative control scheme, high accessibility, low price, and wide appeal offer exactly the sort of gaming experience that libraries should provide: novel, fun, exciting, and social. Just Wii Sports and other early titles, like Super Monkey Ball Banana Blitz, WarioWare: Smooth Moves, Excite Truck, and Super Smash Bros. Brawl, combine to provide appealing and engrossing play options for a wide audience. Now we just have to wait for Mario Kart Wii. Just the phrase gives me chills. Seriously.

3.3.5   PC Gaming and the Nightmare of the Upgrade Cycle

You already know that this book is primarily about console gaming, but I think I should take a few paragraphs to explain why. PC gaming is a big thing, with sales of some top games rivaling the sales of top console games. But unlike the simplicity of the console market, where a GameCube is a GameCube, the term "PC" does not refer to a single device; instead, it refers to an enormous amalgam of manufacturers, standards, upgrades, video cards, viruses, operating systems, critical updates to operating systems, resource address conflicts, reboots, and oh so much more. To get a console game to run, you just need to insert the disc. With a PC, it's rarely that easy, although sometimes you get lucky.

First, there's the issue of hardware compatibility, which you can see evidenced by the hidden, small-print tomes on a PC game box that tell you the bare minimum needed to run it. You then need to get it installed, which can be a daunting exercise in itself, including necessary driver upgrades for your video card or the operating system, plus having to deal with elaborate and deceptive copy-protection schemes, some of which stay resident on your computer forevermore watching everything you do, while others are suspected of being in thrall to the Russian mafia. I'm not kidding.

PC gamers are early adopters, so the market dynamics don't offer much support for older machines or even older video cards. As opposed to the console performance curves, which make single big jumps every five to six years, the performance, and therefore the demands, of new PC games are continually increasing. Many hard-core PC gamers expect to upgrade just their video card every twelve to eighteen months, usually at a console-like cost!

It's very difficult and expensive to maintain an up-to-date PC gaming rig, especially if that's not really your thing. The market is built on people who have large disposable incomes and don't mind constant upgrade pressure—and those terms are rarely applied to libraries! The best chance for libraries is to offer slightly older games on older PCs. The only catch is that if the game or the other technologies it depends on are no longer supported, you may be stuck if you run into trouble.

If you do have a training center that you're itching to put to use with this audience, you may wish to try other game-related activities instead of trying to get something hot and new to run. For example, you could have a level-creation contest for an older game or a machinima show, or you could allow your players to create their own RPGs using some of the simple game-building tools out there. This also plays up the cognitive and learning aspects of gaming, so it may be a good addition to a tournament series, especially when trying to dispel the gaming = prurience idea.

3.4 Accessories, Cabling, Televisions, and Other Equipment

It's easy to forget about cabling when costing out a gaming kit, but if you have several stations and need to make some long stretches, it can add up. When you're deciding what to buy, be sure to think about where things are likely to go in your room (see section 6.3) and make sure things that need to be connected together will reach! Here are a few areas to consider.

3.4.1 Regular Controllers

Be sure to buy enough controllers to have one for every controller port on your consoles. You don't want your tournaments or play time per player to be limited by the absence of enough controllers. Naturally, each console usually only includes a single controller, so you'll want to buy as many as three more for each console you buy. It may be tempting to buy a cheaper, aftermarket controller made by a third party, or even a used or reconditioned controller. But while consoles are relatively safe to buy reconditioned, you should try to buy only new, first-party controllers. Most knockoffs are either lower quality or loaded with unnecessary features that will just get in the way later.

If controllers are a limiting cost for your initial purchase, they're an easy corner to cut to a certain degree. I wouldn't reduce the number of consoles you can buy in order to be able to afford to get four controllers for each. However, two controllers per console is a kit-starting minimum, and it's an easy sell if you're buried in success later and need to increase your capacity cheaply.

Also, avoid wireless controllers except if they're the easiest solution to a cabling problem. They're far easier to steal, and most aren't intended to exist in a room with more than four controllers; you might run into interference or accuracy problems if you've got a full room.

You may want to get controllers in different colors to make it easier to tell which one is which during a tournament, although I just put P1, P2, P3, or P4 labels on my controllers so that players are sure to pick up the assigned one during a tournament, and that has been working just fine.

3.4.2 Specialized Controllers

In addition to the regular controllers, some games will support or require the use of specialized controllers, especially rhythm games. There are Guitar Hero's Gibson Mini SG controller, the Donkey kongas, the drum for Taiko Drum Master, light guns, steering wheels, microphones, and even arcade-style joysticks that re-create the feel of vintage arcade cabinets for retro or fighting games. You may also need dance pads, which I'll get to in the next section.

In most cases, games that require a special controller will include one, leaving you to shell out for another. Most of these games will have multiplayer modes that make it worthwhile to procure extra controllers; a second Guitar Hero guitar or a full complement of four sets of Donkey kongas can make for some fantastic events. For specialized controllers too, avoid aftermarket or third-party replacements. They are rarely as good as the original controllers and usually only slightly less expensive. Never buy a third-party controller without searching for some reviews first; you could wind up with an expensive lemon.

A steering wheel is a fun addition, but it is rarely necessary and may unfairly decrease the performance of unaccustomed players. An arcade stick, however, can be a fun and worthwhile investment if you have end-of-year funds or other such luxuries. The XGaming X-Arcade dual is simply a fantastic piece of hardware, works with most modern consoles, really delivers outstanding arcade feel for retro games, and is often preferred by fighting game experts, especially on titles that began in the arcades.

You may also want to purchase a few controller extension cables to allow for flexibility in tight situations. They're not expensive and can solve some tough setup problems. Remember that they're specific to each console, can be chained together, and you can usually trust the cheap ones.

Finally, some players are going to insist on bringing their own controllers no matter how pristine and well maintained the house controllers are. Don't take it personally, they're just control freaks.

3.4.3 Dance Pads

DDR is the one game your library should be sure to offer, and choosing the right pad is a critical part of assembling that kit. There are essentially three classes of dance pad: the cheap, low-end floppy pads, the midrange hard foam pads, and the high-end arcade-style pads.

Floppy pads are often bundled with a DDR game or available everywhere for about $20. They're OK for a first event or two, but you want to avoid using them if at all possible. First, they don't stay in place while the players are dancing, especially not on high-traffic library carpets. They also deteriorate very quickly and can be destroyed by a single dance done by a larger person on a higher level. Finally, they say to your attendees that you're fine with offering them a low-end gaming experience, and that's not the message you want to send.

Midrange pads, often called Ignition-style pads after RedOctane's highly successful Ignition dance pad, are an excellent compromise for a library purchase. They cost about $80 each, can be found at a store like Best Buy, and are what most moderately serious players would have at home. They can also be collapsed into a smallish box without too much trouble, although that exposes the pad to unnecessary wear. The only catch is that they can still slide around a little and that players cannot wear their shoes to play on them. They will also deteriorate eventually, although they last much, much longer than floppy pads. If you do purchase Ignition-style pads and have a place to store them unfolded, you may wish to look into some of the fan-developed Ignition modifications that can be found on www.ddrfreak.com that allow you to build a hard base into the bottom of the hard foam pad, decreasing sliding and extending the life of the pad.

Finally, if you want a durable, precise pad that will really hold up to abuse, rain, moving around, and dropping, you should look into arcade-style hard or metal pads. These can range from $300 to $800 for a pair, but they will outlast many sets of cheaper pads and can take a lot of abuse. I cannot recommend the outstanding Cobalt Flux dance platform enough: it is extremely sturdy (they drive a truck over the pads to test them), very accurate, and compatible with several different consoles. Another nice feature is that the control cables are a standard computer monitor cable, so you can also get an inexpensive twenty-five-foot extension cable. AADL has used theirs indoors and outdoors for players of all skill levels, and they do the job with grace and aplomb. Also, players can wear their shoes without trouble, although they may have a harder time staying centered due to the Cobalt Flux's lower profile. No matter which pad you choose, you will have some complaints, especially as your audience is getting acclimated to your choice.

DDR can also carry with it its own set of cabling challenges. You'll usually only have one station with two pads, so the scope of the setup isn't as much of an issue, but arranging the pads, console, and projector correctly can require some awkward feats of cabling ingenuity. The best tool for solving this equation is again a set of controller extension cables you can use to put more distance between the dance pads and the console. This allows you to position the pads where the dancers won't interfere with the projected image and without leaving the console in the middle of the floor where it could get stepped on. You'll probably want to get twenty-five feet worth of controller extension cable to have maximum flexibility, and because most controller extension cables are only six feet long, you may need to get a few to string together. That's another advantage of Cobalt Flux pads, though: they are more easily extended with a single cable.

3.4.4 Networking

You can find out the nitty-gritty in section 6.2, but as you're costing out your kit, be sure to leave some room for an Ethernet hub and some long Ethernet cables if you're planning on LAN play (see fig. 2). In most cases, you don't need a fancy hub at all; many libraries may even have something lying around that would do the trick. Depending on how your room is set up, you may want one hub with enough ports to hook everything up, or two hubs with enough ports to hook up each one to half the room and to each other. Know that for this purpose, Ethernet hubs and Ethernet switches are essentially interchangeable, and there's no way you should need to spend more than $50 on a hub or switch with up to twelve ports.

You'll also need enough Ethernet cables to run from each station to the hub; buy them online and you'll save a lot of money over retail. All you need are Cat5-rated cables. Don't spend more for Cat5e or Cat6.

3.4.5 Video and Cabling

If you're going to be buying televisions, the most important thing is to get all the same kind to avoid whining about "the good TV." Check out discount places or warehouse clubs, and if you are going to do any multiplayer games (and of course you are), consider a twenty-inch-diagonal screen pretty much a minimum. You don't need any fancy features, although component input is nice to have (see section 6.1), and a flat tube is a good feature too. If you've got a grant or other source of deep pockets, it's very

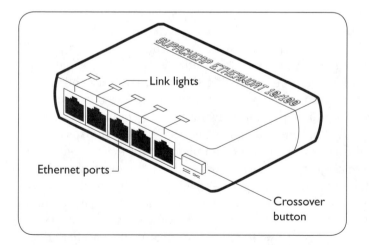

Figure 2
Ethernet hub

nice to be able to have flat-screen TVs, especially when it comes time to set up, take down, or move around. They look slick too. Just remember that computer monitors won't work with most consoles without special equipment or cables; you need a television.

If you're doing one console per TV, you likely won't need any additional cabling with the console right next to the TV, but if you want to take advantage of your TV's S-Video or component inputs, you may need to buy a new A/V cable for your console that has S-Video or component ends. You may want to purchase universal A/V cables that work with more than one type of console to have maximum flexibility. You will find more about this in detail in section 6.1.

If you're using any projectors, you may need to get some video extension cables to allow you some flexibility when arranging the projector and console, especially if you have a ceiling-mounted projector with an inconveniently located wall plate. You can get S-Video or composite video extension cables at Radio Shack or even Target; the people there may even be able to help you a little with this one, maybe.

3.4.6   Cable Management

There's more about this in section 6.4, but you may want to consider a little investment in some cable management tools such as rubber floor channels or even just Velcro ties. If you have long cable runs, you might want a few cheap plastic reels or winding devices to make setup and take-down easier. This isn't a critical part of your initial investment, but keep it in mind as a solution to problems that come up later.

3.4.7   Storage and Transportation

You certainly don't have to spend a dime on this. For months, I carried eight GameCubes around in a cardboard apple box bearing a Post-It labeled "Personal Growth" left over from a shelving move. However, if storage space is at a premium (and it always is at a library) and you're going to have to buy a cabinet or the like to keep all this stuff in, order something early, as such things can require long lead times. If your kit is expected to travel frequently, consider budgeting for some travel cases. I have two of the amazing Pelican cases: one holds everything needed for a four-station GameCube LAN, including cabling, sixteen controllers, power strips, and a hub (see fig. 3), and the other holds four fifteen-inch flat screens. If you get Pelican's Pick 'N' Pluck foam inserts, you can easily customize the case to snugly hold any shapes of equipment. The cases can also be wheeled around, locked, and stacked, solving the transportation and storage problems at the same time.

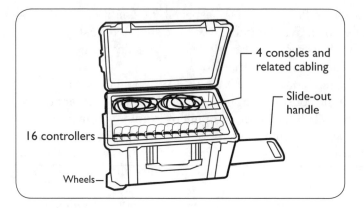

4 consoles and
related cabling

Slide-out
handle

16 controllers

Wheels

Figure 3
Pelican 1620 wheeled case

3.5 A Few Words on Acquisition, or No, Lady, We Don't Accept Purchase Orders

So, you know what you want to get, but where can you get it? Unfortunately, depending on what you're planning on purchasing, and the procedures of your institution, this can be a problem. While Baker & Taylor does sell some videogames, most of the vendors who sell game hardware and software are exclusively consumer oriented, and if you don't have a credit card somewhere within your purchasing process, you may have a tough time.

One of the most difficult issues is that games, like books, don't stay in print long unless they're huge successes. To get some good older titles, you may need to rifle through used bins online or off. While I wouldn't recommend messing with eBay if you can avoid it, it can be a good tool to see how in demand an out-of-print game is. If your chosen title is selling on eBay for twice its retail cost, you're not going to find it on a shelf.

GameStop has a fairly robust inventory of used and new games and accessories available for online ordering, and while they don't take purchase orders, at least you can get many things in one place. Amazon.com also does a lot of business in videogames and takes purchase orders, so if your organization already orders from them, that might make things easier. One other option may be Sam's Club or Costco if your organization has a card, especially when it comes to TVs. They'll usually take a premade library check.

Unfortunately, acquiring what you need likely involves someone buying it at retail store, either with a library credit card, or with their own, and getting reimbursed. If this is going to be a problem for your organization, you'd better work through it early, because you don't want to get stuck when it comes time to make time-sensitive purchases.

You should also note that if you plan to give gift cards as prizes, they must be purchased with a credit card or cash; there's simply no other way. You can't even bring them a premade library check. The bottom line is that if you don't have access to a credit card that you can use to make purchases for the library or the assistance of someone who does, someone's going to have to use their personal card to make some large purchases. Consider it but the first of many personal sacrifices that you'll make for the gamers of your community, soon to be followed by your Friday nights and weekends.

CHAPTER 4

Planning Your Events
or Getting Geeky with It

Even if you have solid ideas about what games you want to offer, what consoles you'll be playing those games on, and how you're going to get all the equipment together, you will get better results, easier approval, more excitement, and more buy-in if you can fully design your service before your first event, ideally, before you even make the pitch. This can be daunting if you're still feeling a little lost in the gaming world, so this chapter will cover everything you'll need to consider and give a little advice in each area.

4.1 Questions You Should Ask Yourself and How You Should Answer Them, AKA a FAQ!

FAQs (lists of frequently asked questions, pronounced "facks") are a central component of gaming culture. They're comprehensive text documents written by fans about their favorite games, and they endeavor to leave no stone unturned, no question unanswered, and no secrets remaining. In that spirit, here is a long list of questions you may have or should consider in the planning phase of starting your tournament service and some short and long answers for each.

4.1.1 What game should we play at the tournament?

If you want the short answer, it's simple: Dance Dance Revolution. As covered in section 3.2.3, if you don't know how to begin answering this question, just do DDR. It'll be great. The long answer to this question isn't really longer: it depends. It depends on which audience you want to reach, how much time you have, how much room you have, what content limitations you may need to deal with, and what you think about what you learned in chapter 3. Mario Kart, Super Smash Bros., Soul Calibur, Guitar Hero, Super Monkey Ball, WarioWare, Madden, Burnout, NBA Live, and Pokémon are all good games for tournaments. It depends! What a cop-out, I know. Send me an e-mail, we'll talk.

4.1.2   Who should we try to attract to our tournament?

The short answer here is teenagers. Gaming is a big deal for them, and their availability is easy to predict with school calendars and the like. The long answer is it depends: what will you be playing? That's putting the cart before the horse, though, since your game choice will be highly dependent on the audience you want to attract. Are you trying for Eliteg33ks? Stephani3s? Bos? Adults? Men? Women? Kids? College students? Haves? Have nots? Existing patrons? New users? The best tournaments will have some appeal to most of these groups, but you may want to start out with a more tightly targeted tournament, then expand your focus by adding games and events with wider appeal.

4.1.3   When and how often should we have tournaments?

The short answer, from my experience, is a Friday night and a Saturday and Sunday afternoon once a month, plus afternoons during school breaks. Your situation may well be different, especially depending on how much setup your stuff requires and the layout of your room and its availability. You could try every afternoon for a week, or every Monday for a month, or alternating Tuesdays and Thursdays. Obviously this is highly dependent on several available resources, but the one wrong answer to this question is "once to see if it works." Give it a chance to develop; never plan just a single tournament. I recommend scheduling at least six events, even if they're months—or days—apart.

4.1.4   How many players may attend?

The short answer here is it's up to the fire marshal. What's the fire code for the room that you'll have your event in? I've never turned away anyone from an event due to capacity (AADL's room is rated for 132), although I've come very close, but it can take some time to learn to handle a large crowd at such an interactive event. You may decide to cap your attendance and maybe even require preregistration to allow people to get guaranteed attendance. There's more on this in section 7.1, but the fire code isn't really the only variable here. It's also how much time you have, how many stations you have, and how many rounds you want each player to be able to play.

4.1.5   What will we do if too many people show up?

Well, you could start by rejoicing in your success! This is a great problem to have. However, if your tournament or your room is full, or if it's simply too late to add someone to the bracket, there's only one thing to say: "We're sorry, but the tournament is full." Latecomers are already cringing expecting this, so it shouldn't come as a shock. Often the kid will be fine with it, and the parent (who may be the reason their kid was too late) is the one who gets really bent out of shape. The best you can do is apologize, sympathize, and let them know when your next tournament is.

You may also want to consider only using half the stations in the room for the tournament itself and the other half for open play. I tend to do this for smaller tournaments for younger kids. In this way, if the little kids come too late, they can still play some games; they just can't be in the tournament.

4.1.6   What's in it for them?

The short answer here is a minimum of $30 for first prize, $20 for second, and $10 for third prize. You can always give more, of course, and you can get away with less in a pinch, but those small prizes are enough to get gamers through the door to discover how cool the events are. With events for younger kids, I always try to have tiny prizes for everyone as they're eliminated, even if they are just vendor giveaways or bookmarks. There's detailed information on choosing prizes in section 4.5, but if you think that bigger prizes generate more excitement, well, you'd be absolutely right. However, what's also in it for them is some high-quality socialization with people guaranteed to have shared interests, and after they see how much fun that can be, they'll come for that as much as for a shot at the prize.

4.1.7   How should we determine the tournament rules?

There's a short answer, but it may not be that easy: ask your gamers. If you haven't got a good way to ask them, you might want to start with some open plays to find some good ones to talk to. The right ruleset depends on your game, your audience, how much time and how many stations you have, whether you're trying to appeal to the Eliteg33ks, the Bos, the Ome-gamers, the Stephani3s, or some combination. Remember to keep your rules simple and informal, get them vetted by gamers when possible, and know that in most cases you can't go wrong with the default settings of the game. Also, always try to start these discussions with your gamers with a ruleset to discuss; an open-ended conversation will disintegrate quickly.

4.1.8 How should we structure the tournament?

My short and somewhat evasive answer is with both qualification and elimination rounds. Space, time, or stations may not allow this, but it's always preferable for every player to be guaranteed at least a certain number of matches (three is the best minimum) before anyone is eliminated. This can pose a scorekeeping challenge, but it makes it easy to reduce a tournament of indeterminate size to a magic eight, sixteen, or thirty-two players if everyone gets some matches, and you then take the top thirty-two on to the elimination rounds.

If you have a longer tournament, consider several events during the day to keep things fresh and allow eliminated players to come back for the next event.

4.1.9 How will our events be related?

Nice short answer here: a season! Whenever you can, unite sets of events into a season with a championship at the end for the winners of other tournaments, even if your "season" is only a week long. You can include other players in that championship too, of course, but the past winners should be guaranteed a spot in the elimination rounds. More on this in section 4.2, but the more cohesively you can knit your events into a whole, the more they'll mean to your gamers.

4.1.10 How will we handle disputes?

This isn't going to come up often, but it will come up occasionally. First, be sure to establish yourself as inscrutable; you should even declare at the beginning of the event that you will resolve all disputes, and your decisions are final. Be as fair as possible, get both sides before deciding, and if someone is upset with your decision, remind them that the next time it may go their way. Keep your authority over the event clear, and they'll respect it. After all, unlike most of the other things they do each week, they're there by choice.

4.1.11 How will we break ties?

This one will come up all the time, especially when you're running long. Section 7.5 covers this in detail, but the short answer is as fairly and quickly as possible while retaining the right to change your mind if need be. This will usually mean a match in the current game between the tied players, with the winners moving on. This is an excellent reason to have a season leaderboard too; it's an excellent, fast, and relatively fair way to break horrendous ties if you just mention that ties will be settled by the season leaderboard.

4.1.12 How can we handle feedback?

This one's got a nice short answer: a blog. Blogs are dead easy and free to get going, they fit with how gamers communicate, and they do a great job of allowing your tournament community to grow between events. The long answer is that you have to handle it responsively, publicly, if possible, and delay big discussions that come up during the tournament until after the tournament is over. That's one of the best things about a blog: if a player comes up in the middle of an event, saying that he can't believe you made this or that dumb choice, tell him that you'll all discuss it on the blog next week and make some decisions for next time. There's a lot more about this issue in chapter 8, but just remember that making this an interactively developed service will pay off big-time in terms of buy-in and feelings of inclusion and empowerment and other words directors and boards like to hear.

4.1.13 How should we set up the room?

You get a big fat it depends on this one, of course, but the things you'll want to consider are how much time you'll have to set up and take down, if you have any cabling challenges you don't want to exacerbate, or if you need to be able to see all the screens from a single vantage point for scoring purposes. Section 6.3 covers room setup in detail.

4.1.14 Who should work this event?

Ideally, it should be *you!* Sleeping in beds you've made and all that. As I mentioned before, two people is a bare minimum at first; after you get running, a single experienced person can work a large but simple event without too much trouble. However, this answer depends a lot on who you've got available. Emceeing a bunch of smelly Eliteg33ks may not be your thing, but there may be someone in the organization who is just perfect for this. Also, depending on your organization's policies about volunteers, you may be able to make official use of some of your more dedicated players to help produce the event, which they will likely be thrilled to do. One other option is to consider hiring game geeks (maybe college-age ones) as contractors to produce your events. It may be as simple as taking out a classified ad to find them, and they may even be able to bring their own equipment.

4.1.15　What should we feed the attendees?

Section 7.7 is all about food, but here are some rules of thumb, developed by the AADL youth department against considerable "selection pressure," if you will: offer cheap, crunchy snacks, like pretzels and goldfish crackers, and a cooler of ice water at every event; add cookies, pizza, and sodas for longer events if you can. Be sure to dispense comestibles slowly to keep them all from being snarfed up in the first ten minutes.

4.1.16　When should we open the doors?

Open the doors a minimum of thirty minutes before the published start time of the event, assuming that you have doors to open. An hour is better, as it's during this time that they'll be able to socialize more freely, warm up, and size up the competition. That pretournament time will become quite important to your players: they can arrange warm-up matches (and grudge matches) on your blog before the event so that they can make the most of the day. Similarly, you can let them hang around a while after the event for a little more open play. I try to do this for thirty minutes or so when time allows.

4.1.17　How should we promote our events?

This can be a tricky one, and it's the subject of chapter 5. The short answer is to be sure to hit the free event listings to catch the older generation, but you'll need to be creative to get the word out to gamers.

4.1.18　How should we promote other library services?

Very gently. If you're going to use your events as a loss leader, be aware that these media-saturated kids can smell a rat a mile away. Never hand out a bibliography, never promote college, career, or SAT-related events if you can avoid it, and only scatter around materials that *they* would consider recreational. Step away from the Pynchon.

4.1.19 How do we define success?

Ah, this is always a hard one for libraries, and it can be very tricky to define success for a program that's trying to reach new audiences. There are always the raw numbers, but they may not tell the whole story. Instead of focusing on the head count, I tend to focus on the new-face count, especially the was-a-new-face-last-month-but-is-now-back-again count. My personal favorite is the said-hello-to-me-in-front-of-their-friends-at-the-bus-station count. If you're keeping track of individual players, you can count how many unique players attended your tournaments each year, which is a very useful metric. However, unless you have something to prove for a grant, you may just define success by the buzz in the room during events and the comments you get from players. When people walk into the room and say, "Wow," that's success. When you get an evaluation for the event that just says, "MORE!!!!!!11111!" in the comments section, that's success.

4.1.20 How can we get players more involved?

Very likely you'll be beating them back with a stick. The most enthusiastic players will clamor to help, and there are several ideas in section 8.1.4 you may wish to consider. However, if you want to encourage even more socialization at your events, consider a clan system to encourage them to work together (see section 5.7), and be sure to assign random matches in your tournament so that players can meet new people.

4.1.21 What else can we do with this audience?

Again, careful, careful. You may think they'll all come to hear a gaming-related speaker, but that might be further from their comfort zone than it seems. Let them discover the library on their own; just showing them that the library is able to meet their needs in this way will likely change the way they feel about the institution, encouraging them to explore services they might not have considered before.

4.1.22 Who can we partner with in our community?

This is covered in section 4.6, but schools and community centers are the obvious starting points, especially if you're looking to share a traveling tournament kit. Partnerships are a great shortcut to reach new audiences, as long as you're not partnering with an organization with substantial audience overlap!

4.1.23 How can we keep things going?

Be sure to have a blog to make the most of the time between tournaments, and read chapter 8 for more.

4.1.24 How will we ever get this past the board?

You've got a good start now, knowing answers to all these questions, combined with the advice in section 2.5, but a good approach would be just not to ask them.

4.2 Planning Your First Season

Whew! That took forever! Now I'll dive into some specific advice to help you plan your first season ever. Yup, your first season, not your first event. Starting off with a full series of events, instead of just a single pilot event, is critical for several reasons. First, you're trying to attract a new audience to the library, one that isn't tuned in to your normal promotional channels in the slightest. Word of mouth will do most of the work for you, but you have to give it time to develop, and nothing allows for that as well as a set series of monthly events that make it easy for players to evangelize other kids and say, "You gotta come to the next one." This also protects you from having the plug pulled if only twelve kids show up to your first event and allows you to set managerial expectations for slow, steady growth. Also, the season structure and even the simple "season" label help the players feel that they are a part of something big, important, and enduring. It keeps the kids coming back, hoping that they're in on the ground floor. Seasons are a big deal in the sporting world, but you can define what the term means in your case. A season also implies a postseason and maybe even a preseason, and certainly an off-season, easily knitting all your planned offerings into a cohesive whole with very little work required.

Now, while you can certainly use the term "season" to refer to something short, like a week of daily afternoon tournaments, you're demeaning the term just a little bit by removing its annual period. It's not a super big deal, but you can get the same impact in that case with the term "series," like the afternoon battle series, with prizes given only on the last day to keep players coming back and aware of each event building up to the next one.

Regardless of what you call it, you'll want to decide what events your first season will comprise. Consider using the title that is likely to be your biggest draw as the focus of a monthly tournament, and then try other games the night before or the day after those main events. It's a good way to offer varied experiences to your players while trying out different approaches to see what sticks, with the constant appeal of your big draw powering the overall growth. Your choice of events is also dependent on the space you'll have available, how much access you'll have to it, and how well it can be secured outside of your events. The goal is to set everything up and get more than one event out of it, amortizing the fixed setup costs across several events and concentrating your outlays of staff time, food, and prizes on a single weekend. I'm sure that your audience would like having tournaments more frequently, but this way you keep the events special and expectations high but also keep the outlays manageable. Your manager will like that.

This brings me to the question of when. When should you have events? Naturally, the answer is that it depends. You can schedule events after school or when the teens are most likely to be in the library, but again, that's making a decision based on an audience you already have. There are always plenty of kids looking for something to do after school, but for many kids after school is the busiest part of the day. I've done a few after-school events, but turnout-wise they don't compare to evening or weekend tournaments.

Of course, your building hours will have a big influence on this: you may be restricted or you may have off-hour events as an option. Staffing issues will also likely affect the when as well, although I can tell you I work seven days on tournament weeks. AADL's formula of monthly tournament weekends, with Friday night all-ages tournaments, Saturday teen tournaments, and Sunday youth tournaments, has worked very well for us thus far, and we get no requests for the schedule to be changed. If you're going to do an evening tournament, Friday nights usually work the best, although you may need to contend with competition from high school sporting events. Back-to-back events can be exhausting, but the efficiencies you gain by getting several events out of one setup can make a big difference in the cost to deliver your service.

Once you've found the overlap between your available and your desired times, decide what types of events you're going to host at those times. Open plays are a good way to get your audience through the door, see what they're playing the most, and get more comfortable with the setup. But as I've mentioned before, they don't have the impact of a tournament and can have behavioral and logistical problems that a structured tournament format minimizes. We tend to save our open plays for school breaks, when the players have a lower standard of "something fun to do." Always try to find a way to have your series of events connected or at least planned out far enough in advance so that you can promote the whole series at every event. Even if you're going to try several different games to see what sticks, you can still call it a championship series—the winner will have to show mastery in many different games.

When you're planning a championship event at the end of your series, you'll need to think about how players will qualify for the championships. You can't welcome everyone into the championship bracket; it diminishes the honor. At the same time, you don't want to have a championship event that's not somehow open to players who happen to walk in and discover it. For the first AADL-GT season (I chose "GT" because the letters evoke competition and exciting speed, but they could also stand for "Game Tournaments," I suppose), players qualified for the grand championships by placing (which I defined as finishing fourth or better) in a single event during the regular season. That gave an extra benefit to event winners while guaranteeing a good-sized pool for the championships. You could also keep total score over the season and qualify the top players; this is subject to change as the season wears on, though, so it doesn't deliver the same "Whew, I'm in!" feeling that winning an event can. Either way, you should also plan for some sort of wildcard mechanism. You can arbitrarily give some spots in the grand championships to the player who suffered the most heartbreaking loss or was the most sporting; just use this sparingly but consistently. To handle those championship-day walk-ins, you should also consider a short wildcard tournament before the championships proper begin to pick the best of the rookies and give unqualified veterans one last chance to make the grade.

Your first season is what you make it; just don't miss this opportunity to package your first wave of events into an easily comprehensible, promotable, and buzz-worthy whole. I believe that starting big was a significant component of our early success at AADL. It may be scary, but it's a risk worth taking.

4.3 Packaging Your Vision

With your season planned, it's time to pitch internally if needed and start the marketing ball rolling. Both these endeavors require you to be able to succinctly describe exactly what it is you'll be doing before eyes start to glaze over. It may be helpful to write a single sentence that sums the whole thing up, such as:

"We'll be offering a championship series of six monthly tournaments for teens on popular T-rated racing and fighting games, alongside Dance Dance Revolution tournaments for all ages."

Or,

"We'll be offering a week of after-school minitournaments on four different T-rated games Monday through Thursday, with the winners invited back for the Friday championship."

Or even,

"We're going to start with two monthly Pokémon tournaments for the upper elementary audience, then two monthly racing tournaments for teens, and then two monthly DDR tournaments for teens or parent-child teams."

Include the intended age of your audiences and the ratings of the games if that's a concern, just to close off most hand-wringing about the content. Distill your idea to this short pitch—you'll find yourself using it all the time. You'll also need a similarly digested phrase to help the players understand who will be qualified for what as the season wears on and the not-yet-qualified start to get nervous and forgetful. You'll get many of the same questions again and again (see section 8.1.3), and if you don't plan out these answers in advance, rest assured that they will evolve quickly under the intense selection pressure of the tournament environment.

If you come up with a complex qualification scheme, a chart can help explain things, and if you have an online leaderboard, highlight or otherwise denote the players who have qualified for the championships as you go. Always take time at the beginning of an event to recap the season rules and attempt to head off some questions.

4.4 Involving Your Audience Early

A blog is the best tool you can use to get your potential players involved early in the planning (see section 5.6), but an informal open play event can also be a source of high-quality feedback to help you settle some daunting questions. You can set the tone by being honest about the intent of the event (come help us test our new consoles, or come help us decide what games will be in the championship series this season) and starting with uninterrupted open play, welcoming them into informal discussions after they've had a chance to settle in and play a bit. Just don't expect them to give you their undivided attention, especially if there are games in the room. Kids today multitask like crazy, and getting 30 percent of their attention may be the best you're going to do.

Online or off-line, you may well find that asking questions about the design of your tournament series can elicit levels of participation that their teachers only dream of. You can get some high-quality feedback about the best times, the best games, and the best ideas for your tournament series before you've even awarded a single prize. It's also important to get your ideas out there soon so that you can see where the questions and controversies are. Just be sure to have a framework on which to hang the discussion. You're not going to get anywhere by saying, "So, what should we do?"

You should make finding a way to get this kind of input about your service a priority, especially if you're feeling like you're flying blind. The more you can tell gamers about what you have planned, the better they'll be able to spot the weaknesses, giving you time to address them.

4.5 Prizes, or The Bait That Cometh before the Switch

There are two dominant gamer mind-sets when it comes to how they'll feel about the prizes you offer: there are those who are there to have fun playing a game they love, and any prizes are just gravy, and then there are those who determine a dollar value for their time and the prizes, respectively, then assess their probability of victory before deciding if your event is worth their time.

Obviously, the first group is a lot easier to please than the second, and if you'll permit a generalization, the elementary kids are predominantly in the first group, while teens, with their surly ways and predisposition to thissucksitude, are more commonly found in that second group. In either case, it's always easier to increase the value of your prizes than to decrease them. Little kids may well be completely satisfied with ancient library swag, like a mug for first prize, a pen for second, and a magnet for third, but you're not going to get very far with teens with that kind of enticement.

If you are able to budget for it, plan to provide nice, universally valuable prizes. I almost always give out GameStop gift cards, but Best Buy or Target are equally good options. It's ideal to have at least three prizes for first, second, and third place, and I consider $30, $20, and $10 to be pretty much the minimum amounts for prizes to avoid looking cheap. I generally prefer to offer $40, $30, and $20, but either way that less-than-$100 investment will bring more players through the door than most marketing investments would bring. If you can afford to acquire one nice gadget, like a Nintendo DS or an iPod, for your championships, that can quickly become the most promotable fact about your series (and one to put in your pitch phrase).

It's generally a good idea to avoid cash prizes: you don't want to have to think about where that money might go. Also, if you provide specific items as prizes, it's always best to give your winner first pick of the prize pool instead of bestowing the grand prize. You don't want anyone throwing a match because they like third prize better.

You may also wish to tread carefully about where the money for the prizes comes from. If you have a Friends group at your library, that's a great way to fund your prize budget (if they'll allow it) because it avoids spending taxpayer funds on prizes that go to an individual. Of course, the value of the prize works to draw the crowd and benefits the library more than it benefits the winner, but those concerned taxpayer types don't usually care much for intangibles.

Note that if you have prizes somewhere in your event, you can more easily have some events or minievents that have only points and glory as the prize. For example, in the third AADL-GT season, there were monthly clan battles for the four clans that earned the most points that day, and the only prize for winning a clan battle was a big fat point bonus. That worked because it came at the end of a day where players had had ample opportunities to win real prizes.

Try to nail this down at the beginning of your process; you can always increase the prizes later, but nothing is going to sell the value of your events to potential players like the promise of free money or gadgets that their parents won't buy them.

4.6 Partnerships, Sponsorships, and Other Ships

No matter the scale of your vision, it can be more easily attained with assistance from other organizations, either financial or logistical. There may be independent or small game shops, comic shops, or other ancillary businesses in your community that would be interested in participating in your event. They may be able to loan equipment, personnel, expertise, discount or donate prizes or food, and just help promote your events to their audience. Don't bother with GameStop or other national game store chains; their margins are too tight, and quotas too high, for the managers or salespeople to care about anything else.

The major retailers, most notably Target, are more likely to be interested in making a donation to sponsor your tournament series. Target loves to give gift cards; how else can you guarantee that a customer will come into your store and spend at least a fixed amount of money, and usually more? You'll also see information about recipients of Target's charitable donations near the front of the store, which could lead you to some other institutions you can ask about the experience.

The next step would be to approach game industry companies for sponsorships. Some of the bigger companies will have online sponsorship applications, but they will rarely fund a first-time or pilot event; they want to put their money behind proven successes. This may be something to explore after your first season is behind you.

Grants are also an option, although because of the political nature of most grantors, they may not be all that interested in supporting videogame events, given how often videogames are used as a wedge issue in politics. However, there are a few success stories of libraries using grants to deliver gaming as a motivator to address literacy problems.

Aside from sponsorships, you can reduce the cost of starting your program by pursuing partnerships in your community. If you've got a teen or community center that's more accustomed to meeting their audience where they are, they may be willing to share a traveling game kit with you or have you hold events at their space in return for exposure to their cooler, tougher audiences. While these types of partnerships may not be essential, they really help to sell the value of the endeavor, and it's always easier to pull something off when resources are pooled.

4.7 Keeping Your Feet on the Ground Whilst Reaching for the Stars

There's a universal drive in the game industry, or in our entire society for that matter: faster faster more more *more*. Once you get your gaming service rolling, you should strive to continually improve it, finding new enhancements and efficiencies in the process, adding levels of competition that add complexity and value to your players, and increasing player involvement. Of course, you need to keep the service operating within its set bounds, but many of the best ideas on how to enhance your events don't have to cost any money or even much time.

There are many ideas ways to improve your events, from increasing your A/V sophistication and adding player color commentary to encouraging your players to produce podcasts of news from the tournaments. As your service grows, you may well need to come up with clever crowd management techniques, like spilling the event out of its room into surrounding areas where appropriate, or limiting registration to library card holders.

At any rate, keep your ears open to the things you may hear (or not hear) at tournaments about other games, alternate tournament formats, or even other nongaming events or services that this audience may be interested in. As you get more familiar with producing the events, they'll naturally get more polished and run more smoothly; if things go really well, take it as a sign that you need to add something new! Remember that new formats and ideas can also continue to wring high-quality competition out of older games, or even make a tournament out of a game that might not have seemed tournament-worthy as you were getting started.

4.8 A Planning Checklist, or One Final Tool for Anxiety Avoidance

Just in case you're still concerned that you might miss something important (and of course you will, that's the way it works), here's a (teen-oriented) hierarchical planning checklist you can use as you go. This looks very scary, but you'll see that you can answer and check off most of these very quickly. It's very realistic to go from inception to first tournament in four months without having to work very hard at it; you can certainly do it in less, but you want to have plenty of time to build buzz in your community. Six months is a nice figure to make all the decisions and buy (and get familiar with) new equipment before your first event. Note that there's a lot of stuff here we haven't covered yet, so just keep going. I figured you'd want this to be exhaustive.

Who, What, Where, When

Determine target audience
    Find "vetting" or focus group members from audience

Determine target audience availability
    Make list of potential availability conflicts
        Local sporting events
        Standardized testing weekends
        TV shows
        School camps or trips
        Other community events
    Make list of potential availability targets
        School breaks
        In-service days
        Open weekends
        After-school peak times

Determine tournament location
    Available rooms
    Food/noise constraints
    Security (can you lock it between tournaments?)
    Library hours/audience availability overlap

Determine tournament frequency
    Periodically
    Back-to-back
    Series or season

Determine tournament duration
    Audience availability windows
    Room availability
    Staffing availability
    Equipment availability

Select games for tournaments
    Same game all season?
    Different games each round?
    Two games each round?
    Bonus or surprise games?

Determine tournament prizes

Determine season prize budget
    Regular season prizes
        First place
        Second place
        Third place
    Championship prizes
    Consolation or parting gift prizes if needed
    Special awards or clan prizes if needed

Schedule tournament dates and times
    Book rooms
    Schedule staff
    Set equipment acquisition deadlines if needed

Tournament Specifics

Determine tournament format
    Regular season
        Qualification (how many rounds)
        Elimination (how many players advance)
    Championships
        How to qualify for the championships
        Wildcard opportunities
    Clans
        How many players in a clan
        How clans earn points

Substitutions/roster changes
Clan point bonuses
Girl in the clan
New player in the clan
Special clan achievements
What top clans get if needed
Determine season ruleset
Chosen games
Game modes
Mode settings
Time limits
Bans
Stages
Characters
Moves
Items
Pausing
Scoring/victory conditions
Breaking ties

Solicit feedback on ruleset

Test ruleset at open play or with staff

Equipment and Furniture

Software
Copies of chosen games
Memory cards if needed

Hardware
Consoles
Standard controllers
Specialized controllers if needed
Cables
Video
Audio
Power
Extension if needed
Television or other display
Microphone and amplification for voice or music
Projector or whiteboard for scoring

Furniture
    Tables for each console and display
    Chairs for players
    Tables/chairs for spectators
    Table/chairs for staff
    Table for food
    Projection screen if needed

Staffing

Registration/check-in

Food setup and restocking

Emcee and announcer

Scorekeeping

Ombudsman/question fielder

Volunteers/assistants

Food and Drink

Snacks

Water cooler

Paper products
    Cups
    Plates
    Napkins

Pizza or alternative if needed

Cookies or other snacks if needed

Soda if needed

Setup

Personnel needed

Time needed

Room layout

Dry runs/start-up phase concerns

Opening/closing

Security/takedown

Promotion

 Promotion budget if needed

 Printed materials if needed
  Stickers
  T-shirts
  Fliers

 Web gaming community posts

 Library web presence posts

 Blog posts

 Free event listings

 Postering

 Press releases

 Paid advertising if needed

Community

 Blog or online forum

 Promoting blog or online forum

 Posting tournament results to blog

 Blog leaderboard

CHAPTER 5

How to Promote Your Events
or Infecting the Growth Medium

In order to successfully promote videogame events at a library, you must never forget that libraries have a significant image problem to overcome. You know the one. Even though the bun may be nowhere in sight, it can be a real challenge to get teens to come into your library when they have to walk past a big, rude "NO CELL PHONES MAY BE USED ON THE PREMISES UNDER ANY CIRCUMSTANCES NO EXCEPTIONS" sign on the way in. It's not exactly a welcoming gesture to these whippersnappers, is it? Think about how a "NO HIPPIES" sign might have played at a public library in a 1971 college town, and you get an idea of the near universality and pointed exclusion of the message libraries are sending. Let's face it, we're fuddy-duddies, and in order to get this difficult-to-reach audience into our buildings and involved in our organizations, we need to be cognizant of the stigma that accompanies being spotted walking through the door. That takes cagey promotion in new formats, careful attention to small details, and the vigilant avoidance of uncoolness in its many nefarious forms. With the right promotion and atmosphere, your events can become something the cool kids will risk being spotted in the library in order to attend.

5.1 Finding Your Potential Advertising Venues, Including the Exposed Surfaces of Teenagers

Reaching new audiences is what it's all about, right? Mostly, and it's a safe bet that these new audiences aren't reading your newsletter or visiting your website or looking at your ad in the newspaper or reading the event listings exhaustively. Reaching these new audiences requires you to get the word out to people who otherwise wouldn't care about what's going on at the library. This requires some creativity, and a little money couldn't hurt, but getting the word out successfully doesn't have to cost a lot of time or money if you identify high-value targets for precision strikes.

When you do this for the first time, just make a list of places to check out, and get it vetted by the coolest teen you have access to if at all possible. You may discover that national chains can be much less willing to get involved with this kind of thing, especially if you're trying to get them to post your flier in the window. Some national chains make it a point to have a community bulletin board for this sort of thing, but that front window is the turf of a bunch of obsessive executives at the home office, and they've already got plans of every inch of window space. After you've made it through that list for the first time, you'll be able to scratch off places that aren't cooperative and have a higher-quality list to work from for future events.

Obtaining funding for promotion can be easier if you develop a single-page promotion plan, explaining what events you'll promote, detailing when and where, showing how cheap advertising fits in with not-so-cheap advertising, and noting who you hope to reach with each.

5.2 Free and Low-Cost Promotional Tools, Including Those of Dubious Legality

There's a time-honored tradition in concert promotion called the street team. They're usually spearheaded by a young urban entrepreneur type— you know, with the messenger bag and the tattooed fingers—who employs a number of extremely low-paid lackeys who paper the town with cheaply produced paper fliers, covering all remotely tackable surfaces. They don't do this just to be insouciant; it works. There is an audience that is very tuned in to any scrap of paper taped to a telephone pole or obscuring a "post no bills" sign, and odds are they don't have library cards.

The best thing about these telephone pole posters is that they are inexpensive; you can throw a poster together in Word in a few minutes and print it out at the office at almost no cost, then send someone out to tape them up or put them up yourself on your way to lunch. The worst thing about telephone pole posters is that they may well be illegal in your jurisdiction, and while you may be willing to take risks in getting this program started, flagrant disregard of city ordinances probably isn't on the table. However, it's worth looking into if there is a high-pedestrian area nearby where you've seen surly teenagers lurking about. I was delighted to find that Ann Arbor had an ordinance that essentially said, "Posters on telephone poles are illegal, unless you take down the out-of-date ones." Of course, street teams cannot care less about this ordinance, so there are always plenty of out-of-date fliers we can take down as we put ours up. It's not just promotion, it's urban renewal!

If postering is not an option for you, there are other ways to use the same cheaply produced fliers. Many businesses will have bulletin boards or post fliers in shopwindows. You may well already be doing this for other events at the library. To reach a gaming audience, focus on the relevant businesses like videogame or comic book shops if you have them. Music stores, clothing stores you'd never set foot in otherwise, party stores, and especially cheap food outlets like sub shops, burrito places, pizza joints, or cafés are likely candidates. You may also try quarter-page fliers that can be stacked by the register. If you go to any of these places and see stacks of stuff by the register, you've found a sweet spot.

5.3 Not-So-Free or Low-Cost Options, or Promotion as Money Pit

It's also worth considering more traditional promotional channels if you can scare up some funding. These events have a tendency to self-promote, but it can definitely pay off to invest in some advertising as things are getting rolling to build critical mass quickly. Some libraries have partnerships with the local cable franchise to get spots for very low production and airtime costs; your library may even be able to get ads produced as public-service announcements and get the airtime for free. Other nonprofits in your community may already be advertising on television and can help you get in the door. One of the best things about cable advertising is that you can very tightly target your ads to specific channels (although that may be more expensive). Good channels to reach gamers would include Nickelodeon, MTV and MTV2, and Cartoon Network, especially during their nightly "Adult Swim" block, which is huge in that all-important eighteen- to thirty-four-year-old male demographic. G4 may also be available, but it isn't as popular with gamers as you might think, because it's awful.

Newspaper ads are a staple of library event promotion, perhaps because newspaper readers are a staple of library audiences. However, I've never seen a gamer buy a newspaper unless they have a bird. Newspaper ads can be effective for reaching gamer parents, and that can deliver an audience, but you run the risk of the parent saying, "Uh oh, a video-game tournament at the library. I hope my kid doesn't find out about it," followed by a quick dash to the trash can armed with lighter fluid. But if your town is blessed by an altweekly (or even an altmonthly), this may be a good place for you to spend a little money. A good rule of thumb here would be not to advertise in any newspaper that doesn't ask you about the cover charge of your event.

One other promotional tool that may be worth investigating is those slides they show at the movie theaters before the lights go out. Depending on the size of your market, this advertising may be surprisingly affordable, and the movie theaters are usually a sweet spot for a certain type of nonlibrary user. In our case, one of the local theaters gave us a special rate on their video preshow advertising, which allowed us to hit all sixteen screens, all day long as part of a fifteen-minute rotation, for about $200 a week. We could also update the ad every other week at no added cost, to keep it as current as possible. We were able to produce the ad ourselves, but they will often have services to help with this too, and if the theater is still just doing slides, that can be very inexpensive. We got the most new players from the twenty-something demographic at our events that were advertised at the movie theaters.

Finally, don't underestimate the effectiveness of a direct mail campaign, especially if you have a good mailing list. While this does not generally reach teenagers, it's a sure hit for parents who are usually delighted to find something in their mailbox that is not a bill and can work very well to jump-start a kids' tournament series.

5.4 Style and Branding, or Avoiding the Deadly Whiff of Cheesiness

Now, one could certainly fire up Print Shop and produce a perfect flier for a gaming event, complete with that cute bookshelf border (this is at a library after all), that kicky Comic Sans font, and that clip art of a smiling sun, because who doesn't like to beat the heat? OK. Put down the mouse and step away from the computer. The only thing worse than gamers not knowing about your event is gamers thinking that your event is lame. Having a tournament in the first place has cachet attached to it, but we have to realize that enthusiasm for the library bears a strong social stigma among teenagers, and their first assumption about a tournament at the library may be that it would be *lame.* When producing your own promotional materials to save money, be very aware of the lame factor and second-guess your stylistic choices, vetting them with a teenager if possible.

Keep in mind that the gamer audience, especially the teenagers, is positively soaking in high-quality promotional materials all day every day. They may not know a Pantone from a ham bone, but they know good design when they see it, and more ominously, they know cheesy design at a glance. It can seem daunting, but here's an easy list of dos and don'ts to follow when producing promotional materials:

DON'T use Comic Sans, Arial, Helvetica, Courier, Times New Roman, Verdana, or Tahoma fonts to make your poster. They say cheesy and they say school, and you don't want to evoke either of those mind-sets.

DO use stylish, tech-inspired, or pixel fonts, such as anything from the Techno section at www.dafont.com, most stuff at blambot.com, or some of the amazing stuff at chank.com.

DON'T use any clip art that came with your computer or that you bought at the grocery store.

DO use the original, high-quality art from the Arcade Art Library at localarcade.com.

DON'T use full sentences, punctuation, or the word "fun."

DO write like a poster for a boxing match, using words like "intense," "mayhem," and "undisputed champion."

DON'T use a border; it's a waste of precious space and looks lame.

DO use solid black bars to set off the top and bottom or as background for white text.

DON'T use the word "library" other than when giving the location of the event. They don't care yet who's producing the event.

DO use the word "free" and mention the prizes prominently.

DON'T use the library logo or any logo that includes the word "teen."

DO use the logos of any local sponsors or of the games or systems you'll be playing.

Another way to keep the promotion costs down is to develop a template for these fliers and just change the relevant bits for each event. This not only saves time but also gives your promotion a consistent look and starts to provide visual cues to viewers from a greater distance. Along these lines, consider coming up with a distinct brand for your game tournaments that gives them their own promotional life without so much

Figure 4
AADL-GT poster

library image baggage. It can be as simple as adding "GT" to your acronym and using a cool font; make it white on a black rectangle and you've got a pretty passable logo. Having a logo for your game tournaments also opens up possibilities for T-shirts, stickers, mint tins, bracelets, and more. (See fig. 4.)

5.5 Reaching Communities on the Web, or Finding the Rocks the Fanboys Are Under

For any game you consider basing a tournament on, there is a community of completely fanatical geeks to go with it. As you may have noticed, the

Internet is a wonderful place for groups of completely fanatical geeks to congregate and obsess about the minutiae of their passions. If you can find those places for the games you'll be using in your tournaments, you'll find a fast, free, and relatively simple place to promote your events to the people who would be the most interested in them.

Now, before I set you loose upon these havens of geeky revelry, a word of caution: these places are often frequented by users who scour the forums for posts to criticize or ridicule. If you make a post about one of your events, don't expect all the responses to be sunshine and moon-beams. Someone in that community is going to say that your event sucks because it fails to account for blah blah blah, or how can anyone be interested in a tournament that doesn't adhere to the fan-made regulations that clearly state yadda yadda yadda? Don't worry about this; in fact, you can consider it a preview of what you might hear at the event itself. However, most of these boards will have sections specifically intended for announcing tournaments, so you should not hesitate to use them for their intended purpose, despite the fact that some dorkus from halfway around the world is going to tell you your event "suxx." You can find some fan communities listed in section 9.3.

While these boards can be good places to get ideas, they are usually highly hostile to "n00bs," and god help you if you ask a question that's listed in their site FAQ or you overlook a stipulation in a "READ THIS BEFORE POSTING" sticky thread. For feedback, the best thing to do is start your own online community as detailed in section 8.1, but posting about your event on an established fansite is a great way for the fans in your community to find out about your events. Then they can become insufferable jerks to all the less experienced players on your own blog!

I'm painting a dire picture here, but you have to be aware that this element is a significant one in online communities, and teenage boys, emboldened by the format and free to take their time to compose a truly dismissive screed, are the masters of this dark art. If you get a kid being a real jerk to new players, set the tone yourself by welcoming them warmly (with a sly gibe at the jerk) and consider it a sign of success.

5.6 Blogging and the Power of the Echo Chamber

At AADL, we launched a new website in July 2005 that was entirely blog powered and allowed patrons to comment on any post. One year later, we had over 7,000 comments, and 6,722 of them were on our teen gaming posts. Online forums and blogs are one of this generation's primary communication tools. Many of your fans will visit your blog or message board more than once a day. Not only does this demonstrate their dedication and enthusiasm for your service, but it also provides value for the other players. You can make a single post about an upcoming event and then sit back and watch as they add new comments and value to the post every day, giving other players more reason to come back frequently, if for no other excuse than to check and make sure nobody is dissing them today.

The blog format also lends itself (with a little help from geek nature) to being used as a self-answering question generator. A new player will show up with some little question, which another player will answer incorrectly, only to be corrected by another who gives a link to the comment where you originally answered the question six months ago. And this all happens while you're at home, obliviously watching *Antiques Roadshow.* It's a wonderful thing.

A blog can quickly become a cornerstone of your promotional plans— a place where you can easily get the word out to your most dedicated players, at no incremental cost, and with their participation and feedback. You can make posts not just about upcoming tournaments but also about other things that may be of interest to a gaming audience: new gaming-related items in your collection, the release of a high-profile new game, other gaming events happening in town. You can also just start an argument by asking them what the best game of all time is.

It's great to promote other library events and services too; just be sure to use a light touch and have the tagline of your blog be general enough to avoid making the gamers feel like you're pulling a bait and switch.

The best success you can hope for with a promotional gaming blog for your events is when your players start making posts on their own blogs (or LiveJournal or MySpace or Xanga or the parental nightmare du jour) linking to your posts. Depending on your blogging software, you may be able to see evidence of these links on your admin pages. If it happens, you may want to watch the linking blog for a while to see what else they say about your service or their lives; it can be enlightening.

5.7 The Secret Weapon: Word of Mouth

OK, so it's not really all that secret. Marketers are well aware that nothing they can tell you will have as much influence as it would if it was your friend saying the same thing—unless they were one of those uncomfortable awkward friends who is always getting involved in pyramid marketing schemes and wanting you to attend dull meetings where they tell you that you could retire next week.

At any rate, the best marketing tool you have at your disposal is a player who came to an event and had a really good time. I've seen kids calling friends to "get down here" in the middle of an event; they understand that these events are social activities, and they want their friends to be a part of it too. A pair of brothers came to one of AADL's first events and kept bringing more and more friends and neighbors until it seemed that their entire neighborhood would arrive synchronously, spilling out of eerily matching minivans.

As discussed in section 8.4, it's very important to plan your events, especially the inaugural season, with time built in to allow the buzz to spread, and to set expectations properly so that the plug isn't pulled as things are just getting going.

You can help the buzz along with somewhat cheap but undeniably effective tricks that encourage players to spread the word. Adding clans to your event is one of the first things to try; not only does the quest to fill out a clan lead to raw recruitment, but the drive to assemble the very best set of players in a clan may encourage people to ask expert players that they know, but really aren't that close with, to join their clan and come to the events. You should consider offering recruitment bonuses of some sort: something as simple as 500 otherwise worthless points for each new player they bring to a tournament or even gameplay advantages, like a first-round bye for players who bring a n00b with them. You can even use recruitment bonuses to help address gender imbalance; in AADL-GT's third season, we offered 1,000 bonus points for each girl in a clan. One of the first things that happened was the formation of an all-girl clan, which might not have happened otherwise.

Your other marketing efforts can be put into service helping the word of mouth spread; you might do index-card-size fliers that you only distribute at a tournament, encouraging players to take stacks to distribute, with upcoming events and your blog address on them. T-shirts are also great for this, making it easy to equip a player with a combination billboard and conversation starter.

Unfortunately, this can work both ways. If your event is really uncool, that will spread like wildfire. Take the tone and atmosphere issues seriously, and you can almost guarantee that the buzz will be a good one.

CHAPTER 6

Setting It Up
or More about Cables Than You Ever Wanted to Know

OK, you members of the A/V club, please entertain yourselves quietly while I review the basics of setting up a room for a tournament, including video, audio, consoles, televisions, microphones, music, projectors, and, um, oh right—you have to remember to plug in the power.

This may well seem like the most nerve-racking part of the whole process for you, and it can be bewildering as you deal with unmarked cables, impenetrable television controls, squealing microphones, unfocusable projectors, and tripping fuses. Be sure to allow plenty of time to do your first setup, ideally during a dry run well before the tournament; a time crunch can turn the otherwise meddlesome into the impossibly frustrating. But rest assured that this is easy stuff to learn once you've pushed your way through it a few times, and it will become second nature before you know it. Of course, maybe I'm just trying to be encouraging.

6.1 Console A/V Basics

Videogame consoles would not be very much fun if you couldn't hook them up to a TV. If that big bundle of wires stuffed behind the TV stand isn't your usual cup of tea, the mysteries of connecting a game console to a television can be daunting and arcane. The goal, however, is clear: get the flashing lights and the incessant noises successfully extracted from the shiny disc and onto the screen of the devil box. To do that, you need a cable.

Each console has its own cable included for this exact purpose. The console end of this cable is the easy part: it's a wide black connector, sometimes with exposed metal, that fits into a slot on the back of the console. The other end is where it can get tricky. The cable that comes with the console will usually end in three cables with RCA connectors (so named because they were developed by the Radio Corporation of America in the early 1940s): one yellow, one red, and one white (see fig. 5). The yellow cable carries the video signal, the white is the left channel of the audio, and the red is the right channel of the audio (game consoles have been stereo since the early 1990s).

When you try to hook these up to the TV or projector, you may find only one set of three RCA jacks, and they may already be color coded for you, yellow, white, and red. If there's more than one set (or even if there isn't, for that matter), take a close look at the jacks and find out how they are labeled. Sets of jacks may often be labeled something like "AV1," "VIDEO IN," "VIDEO OUT," or "INPUT1." You're looking for IN, here, since you want to send a video signal into the TV. If there's more than one set labeled IN, they'll be numbered, and you just need to note which set you plug the cables in for later when you're fighting with the remote control. As long as it doesn't say OUT, you're in good shape. If the jacks aren't color coded, you'll see some labeling next to each one that identifies the video input for your yellow cable, the right channel audio input for your red cable (remember, r-ed means r-ight), and the left channel audio input for your white cable. (See fig. 6.)

Figure 5

A/V cable

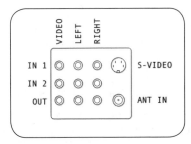

Figure 6

Jacks in the back of a TV

If you are dealing with a very old TV, you may not have any video inputs at all, just a threaded metal stud where you could hook up cable television (known as coaxial or just coax cable) or an antenna. If that's the case, you'll need an RF (radio frequency) adapter (sometimes called an RF modulator) to hook up your console to the TV. This box will take the video signal and turn it into a TV channel you can tune your TV to. These are specific to each console, but they are available anywhere that has a videogame section, and there are also universal RF modulators with A/V inputs that turn into a coax cable. You'll want to tune the TV to channel 3 in most cases, but it's possible that your RF modulator will have a tiny switch to determine whether it sends out its signal on channel 3 or channel 4. If you are using a very, very old TV without even a threaded metal stud, try selling it on eBay! There may well be collectors of such antiques.

Now, a confounding factor is that there are actually several different ways of varying quality to get video out of the console and into the TV, and that yellow RCA cable is called composite video. On the quality spectrum, only that RF modulator thingy is lower quality than composite video. Composite video, while much maligned by videophiles, is really good enough for almost any tournament. They're not there just for eye candy. That said, I cannot possibly write a section about video cables without a significant digression about different video cables and their merits. So, fair warning, you may wish to skip the next three paragraphs.

The next step up in quality from composite video is called S-Video. S-Video is a thicker round connector that, unlike RCA cables, has a right side up and will only go into its socket one way. S-Video transmits the color and brightness information of the video signal separately, resulting in a noticeably clearer, sharper picture. If your television has an S-Video-in jack (it will be so labeled), buying an S-Video cable for your console is a relatively inexpensive way to improve the quality of the image and the event.

Even better than S-Video is component video, a set of three RCA-style cables, usually with red, green, and blue connectors. Component video carries the video's color information on three different cables (hence the red, green, and blue ends). Component provides (almost) the clearest, crispest picture available, with excellent color definition and depth. Component inputs are a bit of a luxury feature on a smaller television, but they're a standard feature of any HDTV and most midrange sets. Using component video also opens up the possibility of a higher-resolution image when your game, console, and TV all support it.

The newest video standard out there is the somewhat notorious high-definition multimedia interface (HDMI), a newfangled all-in-one connector that will be used to connect the next generation of DVD players to HDTVs and beyond. The HDMI connector includes the audio channels, unlike composite, S-Video, or component, each of which comes alongside that pair of red and white audio cables (see fig. 7). Only the PlayStation 3's deluxe model and the Xbox 360 elite model include HDMI output, so it's not really something that you need to worry about in the near future. The only interesting aspect of HDMI that bears mentioning is that the standard is designed to enforce all sorts of restrictive rules from the content provider. It will lower the quality of your video intentionally if it thinks you're trying to view content you aren't licensed to view or if you are using equipment that has not identified itself to the rights holder.

Figure 7

HDMI connector

While this is all good to know (It is, right? Hello?), and gamers will certainly notice if the video is particularly high quality, using anything other than composite video is squarely in the frill category. The biggest advantage of using a higher-quality video signal is that you may wind up with two video outputs from the console—one for the TV and another to increase the value of the event (see section 6.5).

So, once you've got your chosen cable and identified the right input sockets on the TV or projector, and plugged in the cables at both ends, you'll need to figure out how to get the video onto the screen. First, plug in the power and turn on your console so that you'll know when you've got it right. You don't need to put in a game, as all the consoles show a menu of sorts when they're booted with no game. Then turn on the TV. Now you'll need to figure out how to select the input where you've plugged in your console. If you're using an RF modulator, try channel 3. If not, look at the TV remote or the buttons under the screen for an INPUT or LINE select button. Push it and see what happens. You may very well see a little display on the screen that says the name of the current input. If you noticed how the jacks you used were labeled, that should help you know when you have the right input selected. Seeing the console's menu should tip you off too, but it's always possible that cables are reversed or the console's not plugged in. There may also be an on-screen menu built into the TV that is supposed to make this sort of thing easier but rarely does. Some TVs will also go through their inputs if you channel down past zero. Also, if you're using S-Video, some TVs may have a setting in their menu where you need to specify that you're using the S-Video port of your input, not the composite port. Remember that you are dealing with some horrible, horrible interface design choices, and don't feel bad if it takes ten minutes to get the right input selected the first time. Consider it a learning experience!

6.2 Networking Basics

Fortunately for you, networking consoles together into a LAN for multi-console play is very simple and relatively straightforward, and I promise to spare you any digressions on the history of Ethernet or the like. When you are planning to network several consoles together, bear in mind that not every game will support this mode and not even every console has the needed equipment right out of the box. Xbox, Xbox 360, PlayStation 2, PlayStation 3, and Wii all have networking built in, but GameCube requires an optional adapter (the Nintendo broadband adapter, which can be hard to find) to be networked.

To find out if the game you want to play supports multiple players on multiple consoles, take a look through the game manual, or even just on the back of the box, looking for "LAN Play" or "Network Play" or, in the case of Xbox games, "System Link." These are all modes that allow you to have multiple consoles playing in the same match at the same time without using the Internet to do it. That's what a LAN is, a local area network. It means that devices are hooked up to each other but not necessarily hooked up to the Internet or other networks.

If you have only two consoles to hook together, you can do that with a special cable called an Ethernet crossover cable (see fig. 8). Ethernet (the base technology of most LANs) is intended to connect computers through pieces of network equipment called hubs or switches. If you're only going between those two consoles, you can skip the hub and plug one end of the crossover cable into the network jack on one console, and the other end into the network jack on the other console. Ethernet crossover cables will only work to connect two consoles directly, so if you get one, be sure to label the cable well because it won't work when you're connecting a console to a hub.

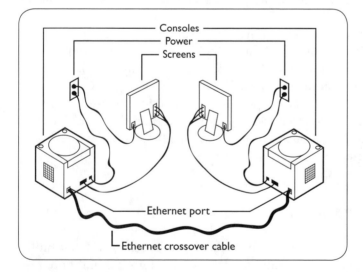

Figure 8
Two-station LAN

To network more than two consoles is a little more complicated. First, you'll need an Ethernet hub or an Ethernet switch ("hub" and "switch" are equivalent for our purposes) with enough ports on it for the number of consoles that you want to network. Be sure to check your game and see how many consoles it supports; again, it should say on the box, but some games will support only two consoles, and some will support sixteen or more. You'll also need a regular Ethernet cable (may be labeled Cat5, Cat5e, or Cat6) for each console that will reach to wherever your hub will go and additional Ethernet cables to hook the hubs together if you need more than one. Purchase these cables by mail if you can; they're notoriously expensive at retail stores.

Obtaining an Ethernet switch is easy: you can find them at Target, Best Buy, and even at some grocery stores. The box will say how many ports it has. You'll need a port for each console (see fig. 9). If you're using more than one hub (which you may well want to do depending on how your room is set up; see section 6.3), remember that you need to use a port to connect those hubs together. You can't connect eight consoles with two four-port hubs, because each hub needs to use one port to connect it to the other hub. That's why you may see five-port hubs, intended to connect four devices together with a port left over to connect to the rest of the network.

Now, associated with this issue is the trickiest part of console networking: your hub may only be able to talk to another hub on a specified port, or it may have a button that switches one port between being able to talk to another hub and being able to talk to a console. If there's a dedicated port, it will probably be labeled "uplink" or possibly "LAN," and you can plug a cable that goes to another hub into this port, but not a cable

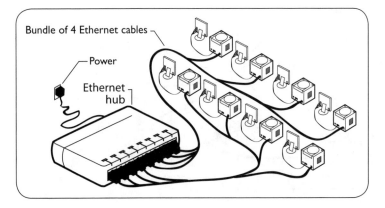

Figure 9
Single-hub, eight-station LAN

that goes to a console. If there's a button, it will have a little line showing which port it affects and probably a little light to show its status. You may see little drawings like two parallel lines and two lines that cross; if that's the case, set it to the parallel lines to connect a console to that port, or to the crossing lines to connect another hub to that port. (See fig. 10.)

In any case, a little green light on the hub or switch (one for each port, possibly labeled "link" or "status") lets you know when you've got it right. If that light is solid green, you know that the hub is connected to the device on the other end of the cable plugged into that port, and if it's flashing, you know that it's actually passing data to that device. Remember that the console at the other end needs to be on for the link light to light up. Those link lights are your best tool for knowing if your consoles are talking to each other, because if they're lit, you're done hooking that console up, and if they're not lit, something's not hooked up right. Once all your consoles are hooked up to Ethernet cables that are plugged into ports with green lights on the hub, you're good to go.

If you've made it this far, the good news is that that's all you need to know about networking to make this happen. You don't need to know anything about IP addresses, DHCP, DNS, TCP, UDP, ACK, MDI, or any other horrible acronyms that you'd need to think about when networking a computer. Your consoles will take care of the communication on their own once you boot the game and start LAN mode.

Bear in mind that networked consoles are not an essential element of a tournament. There are plenty of good tournament games that don't have a networked mode. Networking allows each player in a match to have their

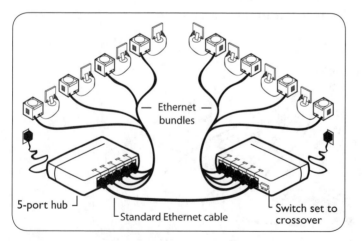

Figure 10
Dual-hub, eight-station LAN

own full-screen view of the action instead of sharing the screen with others. While that is not a requirement, the fact remains that if you are able to offer networked play, you've added significant value to the game beyond what they could get at home and created an image of slickness and competence that reflects well on your organization.

Also, occasionally there may be errors on these networks that can cause the game in progress to abort. If this happens, you'll know it, as all the screens will freeze and display an error message. If that happens, just reboot all the consoles and get into LAN mode again. The hardest thing about reinitializing the network in the middle of an event is keeping the players' hands off the consoles. If they push a button at the wrong time, they may start a game that doesn't include all the intended consoles, and if that happens, you have to start all over again. I usually say "controllers down" until the network is back up to avoid restarts.

6.3 Setting Up the Room, or Forget the Feng Shui

Once you've become proficient at setting up your gaming hardware, you'll find that the most time-consuming part of setup is handling the furniture. Depending on what furniture resources you have at your disposal, you'll want to come up with some combination of the following:

- A six- to eight-foot table for each television and console, with four chairs each. Try to avoid putting more than one station on a table of this size to allow room for gathering and cheering on.
- A few smaller tables—round if available—widely spaced throughout the rest of the room to allow for nonplayer mingling and home bases, with chairs that face the big screen if you have one.
- A six- to eight-foot table for registration and scorekeeping and to serve as a home base for staff.
- A six- to eight-foot table or two for the food and drinks.

Arranging the furniture can be tricky for smaller rooms. I always tend to want to put stations along opposing walls, with the staff desk in the back of the room and the smaller tables in the middle of the room (see fig. 11). Cabling can be easier (and cable runs shorter) if you cluster the stations together in the middle of the room (see fig. 12), but it can be difficult to manage when there's a big turnout, because then there's a big clot in the middle of the room. You'll figure out how best to make use of your space, but be sure to leave as much floor space as you can, as there will be lots of milling about and not much sitting.

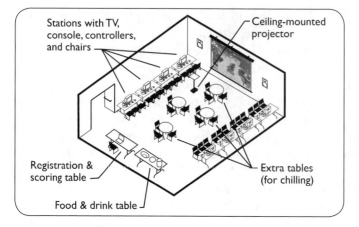

Figure 11

An eight-station, wall-lining room layout, great for Mario Kart

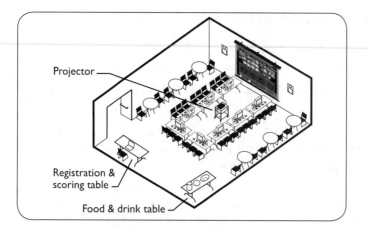

Figure 12

An eight-station, central-cluster room layout, good for Super Smash Bros.

Also consider how you'll be collecting scores. Some games, especially Mario Kart, are particularly unforgiving about how long the results of a match display on the screen, so setting up your stations in an arrangement that allows you to see the screens of all the stations from a single point can be a big advantage. You might also consider tilting your stations a bit to face a central point for a better view. If you miss the scores for a match, however, you can just ask the players how they did in the previous match. This slows things down, but it works fine if you're not able to get a setup where you can see all the screens at once.

If you have a foyer or any space outside the room at all, try to put your food there, as it helps the event expand to occupy the available space and avoids congestion in the game room. You may also want to do check-in at a table they have to walk by in order to get into the room so that you can be sure to greet and invite participation from everybody. Anything not related directly to the game playing that can be moved out of the game room itself will help with congestion later.

If you'll be using a big screen, that will be an obvious focal point; don't bother setting up any chairs with their backs to the screen, and don't put any furniture too close to the screen so that younger kids can sit on the floor up close. This comes up especially in rhythm game tournaments or when you have only one station; you'll want the whole room to face that screen, and you'll want to position dance pads or similar peripherals carefully so that the players don't throw shadows on the screen (see fig. 13).

One of the most important things you can do to prepare the room for a tournament is to make it dark. Very dark. Close the shades if you've got them, and never, ever use fluorescent lights if you have an alternative. Many rooms may have other, dimmer fixtures in addition to the fluorescents; use only those if you can, and consider lamps (or Christmas lights) if you have no other alternative. The TVs and projectors will put out quite a bit of light on their own, so don't worry about it being too dark to play. The big thing is that fluorescent lights say *school* to teenagers, and you don't want them to slip into their school trance. This is the opposite of school—embrace it.

Finally, know that these events may well stink to high heaven, just in case I haven't already made that abundantly clear. If you nail your target

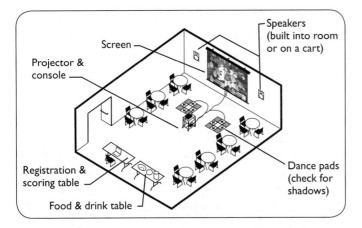

Figure 13
Big-screen DDR room layout

demographic, you're going to get lots of teenage boys of dubious hygiene habits. Even if they're just thumb twiddling, they are going to be smelly, and if you're doing DDR or other physical games and it's a little warm in the room, it can be a real issue. Try to prepare for ventilation in advance: open windows if you can or even a door down the hall. Precool the room if you can (turn the thermostat down the night before) to get a head start on the heat and the resultant smell.

6.4 Cabling Nightmares, and How to Attempt to Avoid Them

OK, so you have your TVs, your consoles, your projector, maybe even your dance pads, perhaps an amplifier, a microphone, lots of controllers, video cables, network cables, and hubs. Not only do all these things need to be connected to each other, but they all need to be plugged into a power source too. That's a lot of cable, a lot of tangles, and when you go to set it up, a lot of time. Imagine untangling the Christmas lights every month; that ain't a sustainable practice.

For a small setup, you may not need anything fancy to handle the cabling, and a cluster furniture arrangement, as shown in figure 12, can make it much easier to get everything hooked up. However, for larger, more complex setups, there are a number of shortcuts you can apply that can save significant amounts of setup time.

One of the simplest things you can do is attach a device's power adapter to the device itself (depending on their relative sizes). Your consoles and hubs will all have external power adapters—little boxes that go between the power outlet on the wall and plug into the back of the device. Sometimes they're "wall-warts," those fat black boxes with the plug built in that wreak havoc with attempts to use every outlet on a power strip. To save setup time and complexity, consider attaching the power adapter to the device with Velcro or a cable tie so they don't get separated and can stay plugged into the right place. Just doing this can take a few steps per station out of the setup process and can keep cables from getting lost. Alternately, you can consider using Velcro to attach the console power adapter to the TV, but this limits flexibility a bit.

After AADL's first few setups, I came up with the idea to put the power, networking, and video cables all into four-inch-square, eight-foot-long, black plastic troughs, including the power strips. We made two sets of four connected conduits that were thirty-two feet long and could be folded into a bundle and held together with bungee cords (see fig. 14). We also used some nylon mesh cable wrap to combine sets of cables into bundles to make things even easier. We would just unfold the conduits,

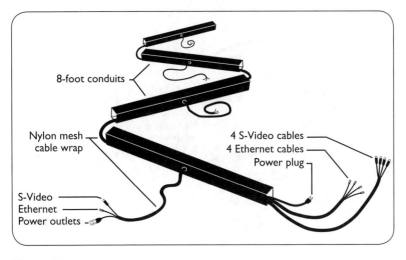

Figure 14
Plastic cable troughs

hook up the connector bundles to the TV and the console, and hook up the bundle at the other end into a single power outlet and a single Ethernet hub. This was a great solution for our normal meeting room and allowed for a very fast setup and takedown. However, these monsters were heavy, unwieldy, and not very flexible for unusual setups or tournaments outside of our usual room. This can be a good solution, however, if you're always going to do your events in the same room and need to make the setup as simple as possible.

After schlepping these things around for two years, including taking them to Chicago twice, they became too much of a hassle. The next generation of this concept involves taking the power strips and the power adapters out of the equation and making two sets of cable bundles of various lengths (fifteen, twenty, thirty, and forty feet) that include power extension, network, and S-Video cables (see fig. 15). The power cables end in a three-outlet adapter to allow the TV and the console to be plugged directly into the cable without the weight of a power strip; we just plug the four bundles into a single power strip at the end. Instead of the easily frayed nylon mesh, we found some one-inch heat-shrink tubing that stays flexible after shrinking, and we cut it into two-foot lengths. We leave six-inch gaps between the lengths of tubing to allow the whole cable run to be quickly and easily folded into a two-foot-long bundle, wrapped with a short bungee cord, and thrown into a duffel bag. This system offers almost the same time savings as the rigid conduits but is much easier to transport and far more flexible to meet the needs of different setups.

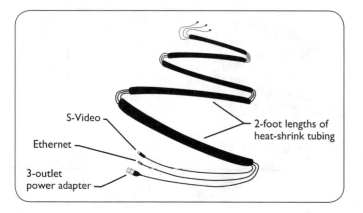

Ethernet — S-Video — 2-foot lengths of heat-shrink tubing — 3-outlet power adapter

Figure 15
Flexible cable bundles

You may often need to run cables across parts of the room where players will be milling about, even if it's just one Ethernet cable connecting the two hubs on opposite sides of the room or a video cable running to a projector. Obviously, you can't just leave this cable on the floor to get kicked out during the middle of the most exciting match of the afternoon. Tape is the customary solution to this, of course, and for that you should try to obtain some gaffer's tape instead of duct tape. Gaffer's tape leaves much less residue and is easier to remove. However, taping down a long cable run, especially one with more than one cable, can be very time-consuming, and even if you use a good, low-residue tape, your maintenance people will probably prefer that you don't tape something to the floor all the time. One free way to address this issue is to run the cable above a dropped acoustical tile ceiling; if you're going to need that cable often, you can just tuck it back up above the ceiling and leave it up there.

However, if you just need a quick ceiling run that you'll take back down later, you can do a tile tuck: lift up the ceiling tile, tuck the cable up on top of the hanging rail so that the tile holds it in place when you let it drop back down. You just need to tuck in an inch or two of the cable for each tile; the weight of the tile will hold it up, and this technique can let you get a cable up on the ceiling and out of the way quickly with easy takedown later (see fig. 16).

If you still find yourself taping cables too often, or if you don't have a dropped ceiling in your room, consider investing in some real cable covers that are intended to be walked on. There is a wide range of cable covers and above-floor conduits available; the small, rubbery beige things that are basically a little hump with a slit on the bottom are inexpensive and

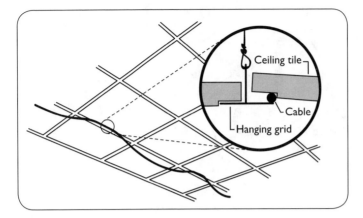

Figure 16
The tile-tuck

easy to obtain, but they can only hold a cable or two, and they often need to be taped down anyway, which defeats their purpose. There are also larger midrange cable covers available that are similar to the beige humps, but you may wish to consider investing in a serious cable management system such as the Cabletek Bumblebee system (see fig. 17). You may even be able to get the maintenance or facilities folks (if you've got them) to get these for you if tape gum on the carpet is the alternative. These are large and heavy, but they are very sturdy, never need to be taped down, and have a huge capacity for cable bundles that might be difficult to cram into the channel of a smaller trough. They are also highly visible for trip resistance and work great outside. Again, there may be some sticker shock, but keep in mind how many uses such an investment will have, and not just for tournaments.

Figure 17
Bumblebee cable cover

One other tool you may want to consider is the magic of a Cat5 balun (see fig. 18). A balun is a little box that takes video and audio inputs on one side and turns them into a signal that can be carried on a single Cat5 (Ethernet) cable. You use another balun at the other end to convert the signal back into audio and video. These little black boxes are not inexpensive, but they usually don't require their own power and can solve some challenging cabling problems, especially if you already have some Ethernet cables in the walls.

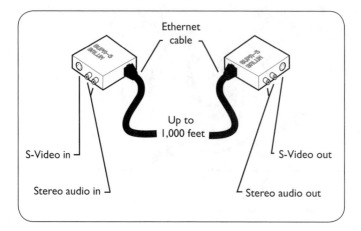

Figure 18
Cat5 S-Video balun

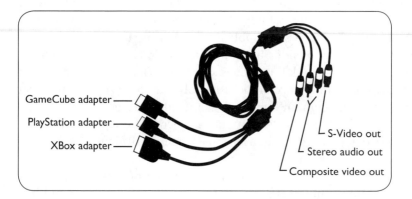

Figure 19
Universal A/V cable

This brings us to the ultimate way to avoid cabling nightmares: have the needed cable runs built into the room! While it probably wouldn't make financial sense to build permanent cabling into an existing room as a stand-alone project, it's a great thing to keep in mind when building a new building or remodeling, because it can be much more cost-effective when the walls are already open and the electrician is already there.

One final consideration, especially if you'll be purchasing more than one type of console, is to get some universal A/V cables that can work with any of the current consoles and usually have both S-Video and composite video outputs (see fig. 19). You can get these at any of the big box stores. Using universal A/V cables reduces the complexity of your setup by only requiring one type of cable and gives you a second video output that you will learn to put to use in the next section.

6.5 Making the Most of a Projector, or Moving Beyond Shadow Puppetry

Ever since the great access-grant boom of the late 1990s, an LCD projector can be found in almost any library. The room you've got in mind for your tournament may already have a projector installed (or there may be one hidden underneath the IT guy's desk in a locked case with a passive-aggressive instruction sheet taped to it). At any rate, almost all libraries have access to a projector, and most of those projectors will have the ability to project video from a game console.

Essentially, you can hook up a console to a projector the same way you hook it up to a TV: you'll find some RCA video and audio inputs and very likely S-Video as well. Of course, the big difference between a television and a projector is that the size of a projector's image depends on where you put it. White walls make perfectly good projecting surfaces, and real screens are even better; don't underestimate the impact of simply letting kids play games they know on a relatively enormous screen. Many libraries have their first tournament using just the projector they already have and somebody's kids' GameCube, and that's a great place to begin. If you have access to enough TVs or projectors to have an extra projector available, however, there are numerous event enhancements of varying degrees of complexity that you can use to add value to your production.

While you can just use the projector as the screen for one of your stations, this may be awkward in terms of room arrangement or lead to disputes over who gets to play on the big screen. One solution to this is to have video from one of the consoles go to both a TV that the players use and the projector for everyone else to see. This makes that station the obvious place to do tiebreakers or finals; nothing builds the excitement like a cheering crowd.

Now, getting that second video feed out of the console is easy if you have A/V cables with both an S-Video and a composite video end or a TV with a video out port (see fig. 20). If you don't have those things, video splitters are available that take one video input and turn it into two video outputs, but they can be finicky and may not be worth the trouble when you could get a universal A/V cable with both an S-Video and a composite output for $10.

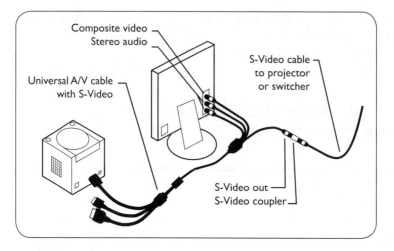

Figure 20
Second video feed

Once you have the second video feed available, you may want to consider moving toward a cabling setup that will allow you to decide on the
fly which of your stations is being shown on the big screen. This requires
bringing a second video feed from each station back to a central switching location, but getting that together makes quite an impact on the event
and gives you an opportunity to have the big screen display the action. If
you have players doing color commentary, you can put them in charge of
deciding what goes on the big screen. It's not that complex or expensive,
but it can really increase the sophistication of your event.

Now, switching video signals can be done very simply by just having the bundle of second-feed video cables in one place with the cable
that goes to the projector, and then unplugging one cable and plugging in
another when you want to switch. Of course, having the cables labeled
facilitates this, but switching often can quickly wear out the cables, or
worse, the jack on the projector, which usually can't be replaced. The
switching of video signals can also be done with a lot of frills and pizzazz
by just having each second-feed video cable plug into its own port on a
multichannel digital video production system like the amazing NewTek
Video Toaster. If you don't have a digital video producer, this is not the
reason to get one, but many libraries include or share space with community television stations that may well have this equipment and expertise,
as well as an interest in producing parts of the event.

Somewhere in between the rickshaw and the Rolls-Royce solutions
I've laid out above are stand-alone video switchers, intended to allow you

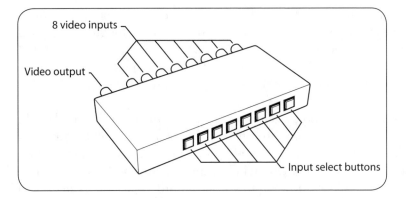

8 video inputs

Video output

Input select buttons

Figure 21
Eight-channel video switcher

to switch between multiple inputs in a home theater setting. You can get a cheap four-channel switcher at Radio Shack for as little as $20, which would allow you to choose from among four inputs at the touch of a button. You can also get an eight-channel one for about $50 (see fig. 21). This is a very small but useful investment that offers returns in the sophistication of your event far in excess of its price.

An alternate use of a projector is to display the Excel spreadsheet or other software you're using to manage the tournament. Your players will have an anxious and insatiable appetite for information about how they are doing, their odds of moving on, their friend's score in the last round, when the pizza is coming, and so on. Having the scores projected will answer many of these questions. Expect that if your laptop is the only place the players can check their scores, they're all going to crowd around you and will even scroll around the screen when you're not looking. If you can be proactive about meeting that need, you'll have a smoother event.

6.6 Managing Audio, and Why Saying, "Test One Two" Means You're Cool

Videogame events are noisy affairs. To keep things running smoothly and get everyone on the same page, you're going to need to periodically punctuate the mayhem with announcements that everyone needs to hear. Not that they'll listen, but at least you'll have done what you can. To be heard, you're almost certainly going to need some amplification. This can be done several ways, from the built-in room audio system to a stand-alone amplifier with built-in speaker and microphone. But there have been times at big events when I've found myself longing for a good old-fashioned bullhorn. That is certainly a simple way to be heard, but it's not the most player-friendly way to get the job done. Taking that route would allow you to skip over the rest of this section, however, so take that into consideration.

If you have an audio system built in to the room where you'll hold your tournaments, you may not need to worry about hooking anything up; you might have a wired or wireless microphone ready to go, and all you need to do is find the On switch. This situation will often include several different pieces of equipment: an amplifier, which is usually a pretty featureless box; a mixer, which often has knobs or sliders; and, if you've got a wireless mic, a receiver for that wireless mic with two antennas sticking out like feelers. Once you get everything turned on (don't forget the microphone itself), you'll want to check your volume levels and make sure you'll be loud enough without clipping (when your voice gets distorted or makes loud popping sounds) or feedback (loud, room-clearing squeals). Here's where you get on the mic with that "Test One Two." Try it; it really does make you feel cool. Try to sound as cool as you can when you say it, just like a real member of the A/V club. When you say it, be sure to say it loudly, as you'll probably raise your voice involuntarily to be heard during the event.

To get the volume right, you may have more than one volume knob to contend with; there may be a level knob on the mic receiver, another on the mixer (hopefully labeled), and sometimes a master level on the amp, too. Most often, clipping will happen at the mixer, so you may need to turn down the mic level at the mixer until you don't clip and then turn up the amplifier to get more volume. If you're too quiet, you may want to start with the mic receiver, if applicable, and watch out for a mute switch on the microphone itself. Hopefully, if you've got a built-in audio system, you've either got someone to show you what to do or a sheet of instructions nearby to help you know what to adjust.

Feedback happens when the amplified audio coming out of the speakers gets picked up by the microphone and feeds back into the system, causing a horrific, high-pitched squeal. This can happen when the microphone is too close to a speaker, when its input or amplifier volume is turned up too high, or even sometimes if someone has closed their hand over the microphone as a low-tech mute. You may also discover feedback-prone hot spots in the room that you can easily avoid, especially in rooms with speakers distributed around the ceiling. If you can't get your volume loud enough without getting feedback, try turning down the master volume and turning up the mic level.

If you have a stand-alone amplifier with a built-in speaker available, these can be much easier to work with. Their downside is that the sound comes from a single place, so it can be too loud right next to the speaker but too quiet in the back of the room. I often use one of these for DDR tournaments to amplify the music, and a microphone, which brings me to my next point.

Adding a second input to your audio system and pumping music or game sound into it is a great way to add polish and coolness to your event. I like to get a cool videogamey-sounding track and put it on repeat as the players are coming in to set the mood and make the event seem more professional. You can find great videogame remixes at ocremix.com or vgmix.com. Amplifying the sound of one of your game stations also adds punch. When you add a second sound source into your audio mixer or amplifier unit, you'll want to test it to make sure you've got the right balance between the music and the microphone, watching out for clipping, especially on the louder parts of the louder songs.

Finally, as you're moving around the room running a tournament, it will quickly become apparent that a wireless microphone is a very nice thing to have. I prefer a handheld microphone because they're less fussy, but a lapel mic (called a lavalier) will work if that's all you have.

6.7 Corners to Cut, and How Much It Costs to Cut Them

Now, I realize that if you were running a tab for all the things I've suggested you buy up to this point, you might be wondering whose car you should hock to hold your first tournament. It does not have to be this way. Making these events happen only requires determination; there are plenty of options to get the needed equipment together without having to spend much money at all.

The most substantial corner you can cut is the one where you spend money to buy things. Depending on the scale of the events you've planned, it can be entirely realistic to produce a tournament using only borrowed equipment. There is almost certainly someone on your library staff who has a game console (and a gamer to go with it) at home. Getting your hands on this equipment can be relatively quick and easy, and it's a great place to start; someone's kids' console and your Gates grant projector can be all you need for your first tournament. Ask the geeks first, if you've got them, and failing that, put out a call for gamer kids. Ideally, you'll get not only access to some equipment but also an enthusiastic gamer who is interested in helping out.

Borrowing equipment can also work for larger events if you're sufficiently organized, and there is actually substantial precedent. Some large commercial console tournaments are done solely with consoles brought by the attendees, although the televisions are usually rented. If that's your plan, you'll need to get commitments to bring the equipment ahead of time and have a system to tag the consoles and make sure they go home with the right people. You may also need to make assurances about replacing things that get lost or damaged for players to feel comfortable bringing their hardware. There's also the fear that someone will forget that they promised to bring their console. This is an awful lot of fuss to avoid spending a few hundred bucks, but it can be done.

An alternate approach is to get the players involved in organizing the equipment or even the tournament itself. There are probably kids in your community who are organizing an impromptu tournament right now; maybe you should go driving around and see if you can hear, or smell, them. If you can find these guys (they're probably guys), you may find not only a source for equipment but also a source of expertise and a built-in audience. You can even hand over most of the reins for this service to the players if you find a good leader in the group; it may be that your path to success simply involves providing space and a TV or projector that you already had. This can be a good route to go if you don't have access to any other knowledgeable gamers to help you get started, but make sure you pick the right person and establish the ground rules for your partnership.

Another route is to talk to local gaming, video, or comic shops to see if they're interested in getting involved or if they have equipment available for borrowing or rental. Don't bother with a large chain like GameStop or Blockbuster; not even the store manager has the authority or the interest to get involved with something like this. The little shops are more likely to want to get involved, and if you're planning some marketing (and you'd better be), it may be that just putting their logo on your posters or fliers is enough to get them involved and maybe even get some prizes, from the swaggy to the substantial.

Finally, if you have scraped together some funds to buy some consoles, you shouldn't hesitate to purchase refurbished units to save a little money. I would stay away from used controllers, but used games can be OK depending on their initial condition, and refurbished consoles have usually been recertified by the manufacturer and may even include a warranty. From my days in computer hardware retail, I can tell you that the vast majority of items returned to the manufacturer as "defective" have nothing wrong with them, so it is often the case that the only original problem with a refurbished or recertified console is that the purchaser couldn't figure out how to use it.

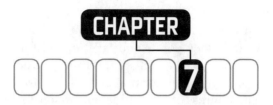

Running a Tournament
or Why the Thirty-third Player Always Shows Up Right after You Make the Bracket

The room is set up, the consoles are on, the lights are off, the projector is purring, and everything is nice and clean for just a short, serene moment. Unfortunately, now you have to open the doors and run a tournament, after which the entire room will look disheveled and run over. As your concerns about setup melt away, they'll quickly be replaced with worries about the tournament itself. Running a tournament is certainly demanding, but it is also undeniable, immense fun and very exciting once you're comfortable with the process. I'll run through the entire gambit, and even run a sample tournament, to give you a few tools to handle common scenarios.

7.1 Preregistration, or Appetizers for the Beast

Once you've announced your tournaments, and the word starts spreading, you're going to have players who feel anxiety about the fact that a tournament will be occurring and they have not yet formally declared their intention to destroy all their opponents. You'll also have parents whose kids pester them daily about your event, and they'll want to get their kids signed up as soon as possible so that they can tell their kids to shut up about it already. It's very helpful to soothe these people by giving them a method to sign up for the event; it can help you know how many people to expect, and they are also more likely to actually show up if they have made a commitment to attend.

Preregistration can take several forms: you can distribute half-sheet paper forms to your service points and take preregistration in person or via phone, you can provide an e-mail address and instructions about what to send, or you can have a web form to submit registrations, forwarding the data to an e-mail address or to a tournament database if you've got one. In-person or phone registration can do the trick for the parents, but it will probably require some data entry anyway, and it seems old school to those thumb-twiddling whippersnappers.

A web form that sends an e-mail is a good compromise if feasible. It looks very official to the registrant, and while it will still require some data entry, it is accessible anywhere to web users and it meets the expectations of your players. If you have anyone on staff who can do a little web work, this is a very quick job; if not, don't sweat it. It's the thought that counts. If you have a tournament blog, you can even encourage preregistration in the comments on a post, which lets your players see who intends to come.

Don't forget that just because someone preregistered doesn't mean that they're going to show up, and you don't want to hold a place in the tournament for someone who's not there. You should still require them to check in (see the next section) when they arrive. You might want to tell preregistrants that they need to show up at the tournament by a certain time (perhaps the published start time of the tournament) to claim their spots.

7.2 Registration and Check-In, or The Queue Attacks

Never actually plan to start your tournament earlier than half an hour after the publicized start time. You need time for people to show up, get registered or checked in, and get warmed up, and you'll need time to get your spreadsheets or brackets ready to keep score. As mentioned in section 6.3, try to set up a registration table that the players have to walk by to get to the tournament room. Depending on your tournament size and complexity, you may need two people to sit at this desk to handle the registration rush.

When players register, you'll usually need to collect at least two bits of information: their real name and their nickname. I've been back and forth about what to call the nickname: "handle" is impossibly obscure to your modern gamer, "screenname" or "gamertag" are tied to specific services (AOL Instant Messenger and Xbox Live), and you don't want them to think they have to have and provide one of those names, and "nickname" may lead them to stick with their real name because they're sick of Grandma calling them "Jeffy." Whatever you call it, most kids will want to provide one, and you should enter that name into your brackets and use it whenever possible. It helps the players build a mystique and an in-game persona, and it adds a layer of coolness to an event to say "Station 1: Doomblaze" as opposed to "Station 1: Mike." It will also help to differentiate between Colin M. and Colin R. and Dylan F. and Dylan P. and Connor D. and Connor B. and Connor A. and Connor U. (Connor is the new Jennifer). Of course, you're likely to have some handle overlap too, but you can enforce that ("Sorry, we've already got a SuperGamer, how about MegaGamer?"). Just be sure that you let the player know what they'll be known as to avoid confusion later.

You should expect that you'll eventually need to censor a handle. Try to be as permissive as possible, but don't hesitate to draw the line when needed. For example, I let "Ur Mom in a Swim Suit" go by for a team name, but I told the player who wanted to be known as "AZN Killa" (he was the Asian) that I wanted him to pick a new name. He chose "AZN Gangsta" instead. Don't be alarmed at this stuff. AZN Gangsta was a very small, meek, polite kid trying to establish a brand that matched his skill. One-upmanship is a central component of these events, as are psychological tactics. Don't let them get away with something offensive, but don't be the fuddy-duddy either. Also, expect lots of darkness and angst. A significant percentage of your players will choose names that start with "Dark," "Doom," "Death," or "Black" and end with "Soul," "Master," "Slayer," or "Force." And try not to laugh or tsk when a thirteen-year-old sixty-two-pound boy with braces registers as "DeathSlayer."

You may want to have paper forms for the players to fill out instead of doing the data entry directly. This keeps the line small at big events but can slow things down overall because you'll invariably need to find people and ask them to decipher their writing. For most simple tournaments, I just open a new spreadsheet and make a column of names, a column of handles, and a column of difficulty levels if needed. I'll do a sample tournament called the Examplery Cup: I've just made columns and recorded names as they come in. If you're doing a team event, you can take the team name, but it's preferable to get the real names of the team members too. Be sure to remind them to remember their team name if it's on the generic side. At almost every tournament I've had a team forget its own name.

If you have preregistrants, you will want to have already put them into your spreadsheet, but with an extra column to record whether they've shown up yet. You can then sort out the no-shows when you're ready to build your brackets. If you have a big line for registration, you may want to allow preregistrants to skip the line and check in quickly. This not only avoids frustration for them but also encourages all the poor saps stuck in the line to preregister next time. There are a few preregistrants in the Examplery Cup, but they haven't all shown up yet (see fig. 22).

Checkin	Name	Nickname	
x	Ralph	Odyssey	Preregistrants
x	Al	Dr. Pong	
x	Nolan	Kikashi	
x	Fairchild	ChannelF	
	Arnold	Telstar	
	Raymond	Bally	
x	Stella	2600	
x	Milton	Vectrex	Walk-ins
x	Bradley	Mr. Boston	
x	Samus	RidleyKilla	
x	Pit	Kid Icarus	
x	Howard	Nester	
x	Satoru	Iwata-San	
x	Cliff	CliffyB	
x	Jeff	Yak	
x	Peach	Princess Toadstool	
x	Roberta	SierraMiss	
x	Reggie	Regginator	
x	Kierin	Ulala	
x	Will	Bungeling	
x	Elena	RawkGoddess	
x	Rodney	Parappa	
x	Marc B.	Foo	
x	Michael B.	Blitzky	

Figure 22
Examplery Cup registration complete

Depending on your community, your prizes, your marketing, and the word of mouth, it may be a while before you have these problems. Don't be frightened by the thought of a thirty-five-person line waiting to register, which probably won't happen at your first few events (although it might!). Be sure to have your equipment up and ready to go at the published time; you will want to open the doors at least thirty minutes early for the hard-core crowd. Let them do open play while you're taking registration, and periodically remind them to get up and let someone else have a turn if necessary. You may want to be sure to remind them to check in, as some players may well skip the registration and head straight for the open play. When you get close to starting the actual tournament, just announce "this is the last open play—we're ready to start the tournament."

7.3 Building Your Tournament, or Brackets, Byes, and Bump Maps

As registration peters out and you get close to the start of your actual tournament, make a last call and then close registration. Once your tournament begins, depending on the format, it can be difficult or even impossible to add a player without it being unfair for everyone else who made it on time. That's why I always start tournaments at least thirty minutes after the promoted time.

At some point, someone will arrive so late for the event that there is simply no way to fairly integrate her into the tournament in process. This is excruciating to libraries, what with our whole "service for all" fetish and whatnot, but sometimes it just can't be helped. There are a few things you can do to mitigate this problem. First, try to exercise abnormally high message control internally in the months leading up to the event. Often well-meaning staff will tell frantically calling parents, "Just go ahead and show up. I'm sure they can fit you in." The thirty-minute buffer can help there too, but try to get the message out to staff that players need to be on time to be sure to participate in the tournament. Having multiple events on the same day is also a good solution, since the next event is usually less than an hour away. Finally, if space and equipment allow, and especially for younger kids' tournaments, you may only want to run your tournament on half of your stations and leave the others for open play so that latecomers (and the easily distracted) will have something to do when they're not in a tournament match.

If time permits (and you should plan so that it does), start with a few qualification rounds so that every player is guaranteed a certain number of matches before anyone is eliminated. This gives everyone an equal chance to play and keeps the weaker players from being finished five minutes into a two-hour event. To do qualifications, you need a way to set up the matches or heats and a system to allow for cumulative scoring. You basically want to cycle through your list of attendees, recording scores as you go, until everyone has had the specified number of matches. However, there are two wrinkles to this plan: first, you can't just cycle through the list in the same order, because the players will wind up in similar groups of opponents for each of their qualification matches. This is unfair to the mediocre players who can never get first place because one of the strong players is in their match, and it's unfair to the stronger players, who may get grouped together (especially if they came in together) and have to fight against each other every round instead of having n00bs to feed on as they're accustomed to. Ideally, each heat will be against a random set of opponents. I'll get to that in a moment.

For our Examplery Cup tournament, the game is Mario Kart (of course), and there are only two stations running in LAN mode, with four players per station combined into a single eight-player race. I'll use a column to record the station (and controller) that each player is assigned to and a column for their score in each round (see fig. 23).

Race	Station / Player	Nickname	Round 1
1	1-p1	Odyssey	
1	1-p2	Dr. Pong	
1	1-p3	Kikashi	
1	1-p4	ChannelF	
1	2-p1	2600	
1	2-p2	Vectrex	
1	2-p3	Mr. Boston	
1	2-p4	RidleyKilla	
2	1-p1	Kid Icarus	
2	1-p2	Nester	
2	1-p3	Iwata-San	
2	1-p4	CliffyB	
2	2-p1	Yak	
2	2-p2	Princess Toadstool	
2	2-p3	SierraMiss	
2	2-p4	Regginator	
3	1-p1	Ulala	
3	1-p2	Bungeling	
3	1-p3	RawkGoddess	
3	1-p4	Parappa	
3	2-p1	Foo	
3	2-p2	Blitzky	
Extra 3	2-p3	Odyssey	
Extra 3	2-p4	Dr.Pong	

Figure 23
Examplery Cup before round 1

The second wrinkle is that many games will tell you who won or lost, and how each player placed in a race, but they won't give you a number of points. If you record "1" for the winner's result in an eight-player race and "8" for the loser, you can't really accumulate those numbers toward a leaderboard that shows who is doing the best. You need to transform those places into numeric scores where the winner gets the most points. I usually use 100 points for first place, and 10 points for last place, and spread it out in between. You'll want to decide on this scheme ahead of time and probably announce it to the players on your tournament blog (you will have a tournament blog, right?) so that you can get feedback and answer questions ahead of time.

When a game gives a numeric score for each player at the end of a match, that can make it simple—except when it doesn't. In DDR tournaments, I always let players dance at whatever level they want so that people can participate with less fear of humiliating themselves. The problem is that most versions of DDR normalize the scores across difficulties, so that it's possible for someone dancing on beginner to beat someone dancing on heavy if they miss fewer steps, even though they face far fewer steps. It's not fair for a beginner to be able to beat a seasoned player, and it also encourages players to dance below their level to try to maximize their score, which lowers the level of competition. So, instead of taking the raw DDR point score, I record the number of "perfect" steps each player gets. This is shown right on the scoring screen at the end of a song. A great player could score 400 points or more; a good beginner might score 60. This is a more fundamental measure of a player's performance, while still allowing for a little strategizing. Our players have been very pleased with it. Other games have similar normalizing schemes. If you're going to allow different difficulty levels in a tournament, make sure that the scores are still fair.

So, once you have a plan for distributing points and players, use your spreadsheet to set up the matches. If you don't have a magic number of players, you might have a match at the end of a round that has fewer players than the others. You might consider padding out that last match with extra players to prevent the other players from getting an unfairly easy match. Be sure not to count those scores for the extra players. One other thing to think about is to spread around level or song choices where applicable; for example, for DDR or Karaoke Revolution tournaments, we usually go through a list of pairs twice for qualification, and the players each get to pick the song once. That also encourages teamwork for players who collaborate to choose two mutually advantageous songs.

Alternately, depending on the number of players you have and the amount of time available, you may want to bypass qualification rounds and do a straight single- or double-elimination tournament. This makes for a simpler overall structure and is more time effective, but it's far more unforgiving for weaker players. In a single-elimination tournament, the losers of each match are out, while in a double-elimination tournament, the losers of each match move into the loser's bracket where they have another chance to move on. In either type, the biggest limitation is that you need to lay out a bracket that has a certain number of slots (eight, sixteen, thirty-two, sixty-four). If you don't have that number of players, you'll need to pad out the empty spots in the bracket with byes. A bye is when a player does not face an opponent in a round, automatically advancing to the next round. While this is an established tournament convention, it can be hard to decide fairly who gets those byes if you don't have rankings on which to base them. Alternately, you can cap the size of your tournament (which your room size may force you to do anyway) and limit enrollment to the first sixteen or thirty-two or sixty-four players for a nice, neat bracket. Again, while skipping the qualification round can save time and complexity, going right to elimination will knock out half the attendees in the first round.

For the Examplery Cup, there will be three qualification matches per player, and the top players will then advance to the elimination rounds.

Bump maps have nothing to do with this section. I am just checking to see if you are paying attention.

7.4 Running Matches and Keeping Score and Answering Questions and Finding Missing Players and Maintaining Order

Once you have your tournament laid out, you're ready to start the first match. I always like to take that opportunity to introduce myself and give any rules for the tournament, remind people to hang on to their gadgets, and announce any upcoming events. Then it's on to the first match. If you have a way to project who is at what station, whether it's just your spreadsheet or something more sophisticated, that's always helpful, but I will often just read out who should be at which station and with which controller. If you will have more than one player per station, be sure to remind the players that it's important that they sit at the assigned controller to make sure that their score is properly recorded. You'll want to label your controllers in advance (e.g., P1, P2, P3, P4) to avoid the mad cable-tracing scramble.

A consistent problem will be players not showing up when called for their matches. They may be in the bathroom, on the phone, in the stacks (yes!), on their way home already, or usually just not paying attention. After I go through the seatings once, I ask if any stations are missing any players and give the missing players a "going once, going twice" before they forfeit their matches. You may decide that players who miss a match forfeit future matches so that there's an incentive for players to keep attentive and for things to move smoothly, but if you're going to do this, be sure to mention it as part of your introduction.

Once you've got everyone seated and the first match under way, you can take some time to answer questions or do play-by-play on a match. The critical thing is to be ready to record the scores when each match ends, as you may only have a few seconds to get them. You might want to jot the scores down on a pad and then enter them later after you get the next match started, or you may want to get fancy and use a tablet computer to enter the scores directly (guess which one I do). Some games may keep the scores up on the screen until someone hits a button; if that's the case, you should warn the players not to dismiss the results screen until you've recorded the scores. If you miss some scores, don't hesitate to ask the players to report their scores, but do it right away: the memory of the previous match is significantly obscured by a new match.

Figure 24 shows the Examplery Cup at the end of the first round, with the scores that each player earned.

As you move through your sets of matches, make columns on your spreadsheet to the right of the players' names for each round of matches. You can then easily tally up the scores for each player across the rows and then sort by the total score to get your leaderboard and determine who is going to move on to your elimination rounds. Now, one problem with this is that your players are going to be obsessed with how they're doing and their real-time odds of moving on, so you may want to get a little fancy with Excel and make a place on your spreadsheet where you can copy your real score data and make a sorted leaderboard after every round. This can be a good thing to project, as mentioned in section 6.5.

Often your number of players and matches won't evenly divide into the number of stations you have, which means that the last qualifying match won't be full. It can offer an unfair advantage for the players in the last match to face a smaller number of opponents. To avoid this, fill out

Race	Station / Player	Nickname	Round 1	Round 2
1	1-p1	Odyssey	40	50
1	1-p2	Dr. Pong	50	60
1	1-p3	Kikashi	10	
1	1-p4	ChannelF	60	
1	2-p1	2600	100	
1	2-p2	Vectrex	20	
1	2-p3	Mr. Boston	30	
1	2-p4	RidleyKilla	80	
2	1-p1	Kid Icarus	30	
2	1-p2	Nester	80	
2	1-p3	Iwata-San	60	
2	1-p4	CliffyB	40	
2	2-p1	Yak	20	
2	2-p2	Princess Toadstool	50	
2	2-p3	SierraMiss	10	
2	2-p4	Regginator	100	
3	1-p1	Ulala	10	
3	1-p2	Bungeling	100	
3	1-p3	RawkGoddess	40	
3	1-p4	Parappa	30	
3	2-p1	Foo	20	
3	2-p2	Blitzky	80	
Extra 3	2-p3	Odyssey	50	
Extra 3	2-p4	Dr.Pong	60	

Figure 24

Examplery Cup after round 1

Race	Station / Player	Nickname	Round 1	Round 2
4	1-p1	Ulala	10	
4	1-p2	Iwata-San	60	
4	1-p3	Bungeling	100	
4	1-p4	Blitzky	80	
4	2-p1	Vectrex	20	
4	2-p2	CliffyB	40	
4	2-p3	Foo	20	
4	2-p4	Kid Icarus	30	
5	1-p1	Parappa	30	
5	1-p2	Nester	80	
5	1-p3	Kikashi	10	
5	1-p4	Mr. Boston	30	
5	2-p1	SierraMiss	10	
5	2-p2	RidleyKilla	80	
5	2-p3	ChannelF	60	
5	2-p4	Princess Toadstool	50	
6	1-p1	Regginator	100	
6	1-p2	Yak	20	
6	1-p3	RawkGoddess	40	
6	1-p4	2600	100	
Extra 6	2-p1	Ulala		
Extra 6	2-p2	Iwata-San		
Extra 6	2-p3	Parappa		
Extra 6	2-p4	Nester		
	1-p2	Dr. Pong	50	60
	1-p1	Odyssey	40	50

Figure 25
Examplery Cup before round 2

that last bracket with other players who get an extra match, but let them know that those extra scores won't count.

Figure 25 shows the Examplery Cup before round 2: I've reshuffled the order of the players by sorting the rows in reverse alphabetical order to give them different opponents. Figure 26 shows the results after round 2.

7.5 Elimination Rounds and Big Ugly Ties

So, qualification rounds are complete and your players' scores have been totaled and sorted, and you're ready to take the top sixteen players on to the elimination rounds. But there's one small problem—the fifteenth through twenty-first places are all tied with 70 points (see fig. 27). Before you can proceed with the elimination rounds, you'll need to do a tiebreaking match to decide which of the tied players get to move on.

Race	Station / Player	Nickname	Round 1	Round 2	Round 3
4	1-p1	Ulala	10	50	10
4	1-p2	Iwata-San	60	80	60
4	1-p3	Bungeling	100	100	
4	1-p4	Blitzky	80	60	
4	2-p1	Vectrex	20	40	
4	2-p2	CliffyB	40	10	
4	2-p3	Foo	20	30	
4	2-p4	Kid Icarus	30	20	
5	1-p1	Parappa	30	50	30
5	1-p2	Nester	80	60	40
5	1-p3	Kikashi	10	40	
5	1-p4	Mr. Boston	30	30	
5	2-p1	SierraMiss	10	20	
5	2-p2	RidleyKilla	80	100	
5	2-p3	ChannelF	60	80	
5	2-p4	Princess Toadstool	50	10	
6	1-p1	Regginator	100	80	
6	1-p2	Yak	20	20	
6	1-p3	RawkGoddess	40	50	
6	1-p4	2600	100	100	
Extra 6	2-p1	Ulala		10	
Extra 6	2-p2	Iwata-San		60	
Extra 6	2-p3	Parappa		30	
Extra 6	2-p4	Nester		40	
	1-p2	Dr. Pong	50	60	
	1-p1	Odyssey	40	50	

Figure 26
Examplery Cup after round 2

In our example, after all players have had their three races, we've got seven players vying for two spots, the fifteenth and sixteenth spots in the elimination bracket. Since our game takes up to eight players at once, this is easy: we run one race for those seven players, and first and second place move on. If you can't have all the tied players in one match, you have to do a few preliminary matches and have the top winners from those advance to a final tiebreaker. This can get pretty horrific if you've only had two or three qualifying matches; the likelihood of a tie (and a big ugly one, at that) is much greater, so it's another good reason to try to maximize the number of qualifying matches each player gets. If you can't figure out a scheme to break the tie fairly, solicit the advice of your players. They'll be heavily invested in a fair outcome at that moment, and you're likely to get some intense participation.

Another option you have when pressed for time is to check the next smaller bracket size and see if you can avoid a tie there. While this can cause significant grumblings if you said you were going to take the top sixteen and you decide you can only take the top eight, it's still fair, and it

Nickname	Round 1	Round 2	Round 3	Total	Rank
2600	100	100	100	300	1
Bungeling	100	100	80	280	2
Regginator	100	80	80	260	3
RidleyKilla	80	100	40	220	4
Dr. Pong	50	60	100	210	5
Iwata-San	60	80	60	200	6
ChannelF	60	80	60	200	6
Blitzky	80	60	50	190	8
Nester	80	60	40	180	9
RawkGoddess	40	50	60	150	10
Odyssey	40	50	50	140	11
Parappa	30	50	30	110	12
Vectrex	20	40	30	90	13
Foo	20	30	40	90	13
Ulala	10	50	10	70	15
Mr. Boston	30	30	10	70	15
Princess Toadstool	50	10	10	70	15
CliffyB	40	10	20	70	15
Kid Icarus	30	20	20	70	15
Kikashi	10	40	20	70	15
Yak	20	20	30	70	15
SierraMiss	10	20	10	40	22

Figure 27

Examplery Cup showing seven-way tie for fifteenth place

can be a real time-saver when there's a time constraint. If you're worried about having to do this, you may say at the beginning that you reserve the right to adapt the number that move on as time permits, but it will make your players nervous and jumpy. Well, jumpier.

After you've run any necessary tiebreakers, an easy way to move on from here with your spreadsheet is just to give the tiebreaker winners 1 extra point. You can then re-sort your leaderboard and easily see your top sixteen. If you've got the time, it's always nice (especially for younger kids) to take as many people forward into elimination as possible, but remember that you must take four, eight, sixteen, or thirty-two players on to elimination or have byes in the first round. Each bye (see section 7.3) leaves an empty spot in the bracket, and a bracket padded with those empty spots allows you to advance an odd (or just not a power of two) number of players on to elimination. Just be sure to give the byes to the players at the top of the leaderboard; remember, byes are only fair if they're earned.

You can see in figure 28 that we have two winners from our tiebreaker, and they each have their extra points. I've re-sorted the totals, and we're ready to move on to the seeded elimination rounds.

Elimination usually works best when it's a two-player head-to-head match; the winner advances. You can do four-player matches and have the winner or first and second place advance too, but that's a more complex

Nickname	Round 1	Round 2	Round 3	Total	Rank
2600	100	100	100	300	1
Bungeling	100	100	80	280	2
Regginator	100	80	80	260	3
RidleyKilla	80	100	40	220	4
Dr. Pong	50	60	100	210	5
Iwata-San	60	80	60	200	6
ChannelF	60	80	60	200	6
Blitzky	80	60	50	190	8
Nester	80	60	40	180	9
RawkGoddess	40	50	60	150	10
Odyssey	40	50	50	140	11
Parappa	30	50	30	110	12
Vectrex	20	40	30	90	13
Foo	20	30	40	90	13
Princess Toadstool	50	10	11	71	15
CliffyB	40	10	21	71	16
Ulala	10	50	10	70	17
Mr. Boston	30	30	10	70	17
Kid Icarus	30	20	20	70	17
Kikashi	10	40	20	70	17
Yak	20	20	30	70	17
SierraMiss	10	20	10	40	22

Figure 28
Examplery Cup after tiebreaker

bracket. When doing head-to-head matches, it's a good idea to seed the brackets. Seeded brackets (like NCAA's March Madness) reward the top qualifiers for their prowess by allowing them to face weaker opponents in the early rounds of elimination. We'll use a seeded bracket for the Examplery Cup, so first place faces sixteenth place, second faces fifteenth place, and so on. This means that most of the matches will have a strong favorite, allowing for dramatic upsets. It also means that the eighth- versus ninth-place match in the middle is usually a very even and exciting match. Keep this in mind as you host the event to maximize the drama (see section 7.6). We'll switch Mario Kart to two-player battle mode now, with each player getting their own full-screen view of the action on one of two stations.

It's easy to set up a bracket in Excel—just skip a line between sets in the first round and work your way to the right. You can save time by creating empty brackets of various sizes in Excel and then opening a copy for your tournament. Figure 29 shows our seeded Examplery Cup elimination bracket, ready for the first round of elimination.

It's also nice to refer to each round of the elimination by name to establish the stakes. You can start with prelims and proceed through quarterfinals to the rarefied heights of the semifinals, when you have just four players (or teams) remaining. Run these two matches just like any other, with the winners going to the final match to decide who takes first prize

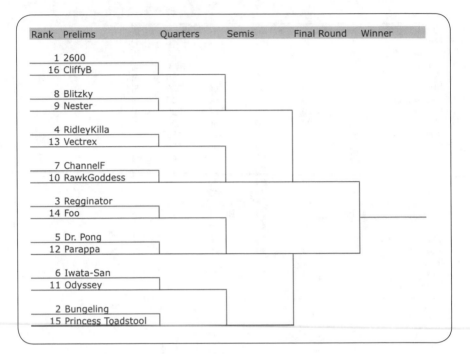

Rank	Prelims	Quarters	Semis	Final Round	Winner
1	2600				
16	CliffyB				
8	Blitzky				
9	Nester				
4	RidleyKilla				
13	Vectrex				
7	ChannelF				
10	RawkGoddess				
3	Regginator				
14	Foo				
5	Dr. Pong				
12	Parappa				
6	Iwata-San				
11	Odyssey				
2	Bungeling				
15	Princess Toadstool				

Figure 29

Examplery Cup seeded elimination bracket

and who takes second, leaving the two losers to face each other in the consolation match (which should come before the final match) to decide who wins third prize and who wins fourth (or goes home with a library mug).

The final bracket of the Examplery Cup shows clearly who won each match and the consolation match as well (see fig. 30).

After you've awarded your prizes, if time allows, you can offer a little more open play before closing up shop. There will certainly be the demand, and it allows the social elements of the event to slow down gradually instead of spilling out into the foyer in a roiling clump.

7.6 A Few Words on Mastering the Ceremonies, or Finding Your Inner Guy Smiley

OK, you've successfully created a circus, and guess what—you're the ringmaster. While a big part of running these events is managing the tournament logistics, getting people seated, and getting scores recorded, it's also up to you to build a fun, cool atmosphere, make new users feel welcome,

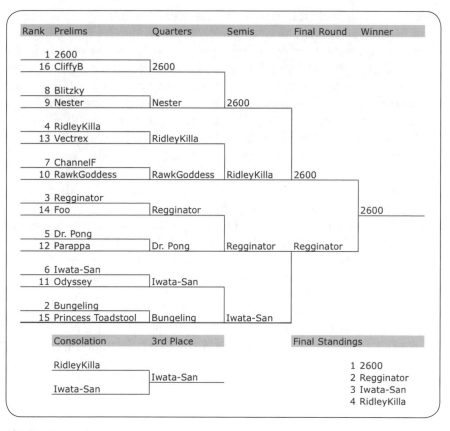

Rank	Prelims	Quarters	Semis	Final Round	Winner
1	2600				
16	CliffyB	2600			
8	Blitzky				
9	Nester	Nester	2600		
4	RidleyKilla				
13	Vectrex	RidleyKilla			
7	ChannelF				
10	RawkGoddess	RawkGoddess	RidleyKilla	2600	
3	Regginator				2600
14	Foo	Regginator			
5	Dr. Pong				
12	Parappa	Dr. Pong	Regginator	Regginator	
6	Iwata-San				
11	Odyssey	Iwata-San			
2	Bungeling				
15	Princess Toadstool	Bungeling	Iwata-San		

Consolation	3rd Place		Final Standings
RidleyKilla			1 2600
	Iwata-San		2 Regginator
Iwata-San			3 Iwata-San
			4 RidleyKilla

Figure 30

Examplery Cup tournament complete

and most important, tell the story of the event as it unfolds, keeping players emotionally involved, aware of the stakes, and hungry for more.

Part of this is your tone and demeanor. First, be sure to introduce yourself using just your first name and be as welcoming and patient with the questions as possible; they will be overwhelming, especially if you are the only point of access to information about how a player is doing in the tournament. Try to remember players' names and handles; nothing makes them feel as welcome as being remembered. Be as informal as possible, high energy if you can muster it, and don't be afraid to use cheesy sports broadcasting hyperbole like, "It all comes down to this" or "This is what we've all been waiting for" or "Two players enter, one player leaves." They'll eat it up, and the central absurdity of a librarian applying such importance to a videogame tournament will keep it from getting too heavy. If the crowd exclaims, "Woah!" or "Wow!" or "Ohhhhh!" during the climax of a match, join right in on the mic. Also, following the excitement of your audience can help you learn to decipher what's going on on-screen and be better able to comment on it. Catchphrases can help fill in the gaps, and don't be afraid to be loud if it's in your character. If this is bizarre and alien to you, don't worry: there's inspiration on half the channels of the dial (what's a dial?). Just shoot more for the roller derby/monster truck announcer than the golf/poker announcer and you'll be fine.

In addition to a high-energy and friendly delivery, you need to find the drama in what's happening at your event and then emphasize it. You'll want to begin by acknowledging the stakes, especially when elimination is on the line, but you also want to emphasize rising and falling stars, power vacuums left by absent regulars, or dynastic and sibling rivalries, setting the stage for an event based on past performance and building the significance of those final matches far beyond that which Mario Kart in a library would otherwise merit. The goal is to make your players feel that they are a part of something big and amplify the value of the glory of victory and the agony of defeat.

I recognize that library events don't often have winners and losers and that for someone to experience the bitter disappointment of failure at a library event may not seem like such a good idea. Keep in mind, however, that these are essentially sporting events, and you'll find few players who don't want to be involved in a competition because they might lose. To the contrary, they'll keep coming back for more because they might win. You can help by keeping the tone positive, encouraging good attitudes wherever possible, and always leading the audience in applause for eliminated players. This can be especially important in tournaments for younger kids who may have had little prior exposure to high-stakes failure. I always try to have plenty of consolation prizes for kids' tournaments; even things that you would normally give away at the circ desk will do. You don't need to do this for kids who don't make it to the elimination rounds (although they'll love it if you do), but once kids make it out of qualification, focus on the eliminated players after each match, give them their bookmarks or other swag right then, mention that they finished thirteenth out of thirty-eight players, and lead the audience in that applause for "doing such a great job today." If you can keep the atmosphere cool, light, and fun, players and parents alike will leave the event with fond feelings for the library regardless of whether they won or lost.

It may well be that you are the person in charge of these events, and you simply cannot imagine yourself performing in this capacity. I admit that stage presence isn't always a required qualification for a librarian, but if you do storytime, you have no excuse! If it's the case that you don't see yourself in the center of this maelstrom, you may look for an internal assistant or even a charismatic player to enlist in this role. At AADL we actually have to have auditions for our color commentary people. The players want to do this, and if you can clearly outline what you expect, it can work out well and really create a great relationship between the library and the commentators. However, don't psych yourself out: your willingness to try this will make a big impact on your players. From my own experience, the relationship I've built with our players by being right there in the middle of the event, keeping things running and exciting, has allowed us to build mutual respect and admiration that is simply hard to come by, especially with teens who are most accustomed to acrimonious, or at best indifferent, relationships with adults. If you can find that kernel of a game show host inside yourself, it can be the key to a higher level of kinship with your players and all the benefits that will bring to your institution.

7.7 Food, or Why the Pizza Guy Had Better Be Punctual

I don't think I would go so far as to say that tasty comestibles are an essential part of hosting a tournament, but if you could only add one frill, this would be the one. Having food at your event demonstrates to your players that you are committed to the purely recreational value of the event: you never get to eat in class unless you're making ice cream or building Mount Kilimanjaro out of graham crackers for a project. You don't have to go far to feed your audience depending on the length of your event. At shorter (up to three-hour) events, you can get by with a few bags of pretzels, goldfish, and store-brand cookies and a big cooler of ice water. Add cups, small paper plates, and napkins, and you're pretty much set. It's nice to add apples or bananas, albeit a little optimistic for a teen event, but once the other stuff is gone, they will indeed eat fruit. Another option to consider is a small commercial popcorn machine stocked with a supply of corn, oil packets (yuck!), and bags. The cost of the supplies to feed popcorn to people at a single event is very low, and it can find an application in all other sorts of library events too.

At a shorter event, you shouldn't need to bother with soda (pop? Coke? Please insert your regional euphemism for soft drink here); ice water will do the trick, and at a DDR or other physical game tournament, water is essential. "Teen Faints from Exhaustion While Playing Degenerate Videogames at Public Library" is obviously not the type of coverage you're looking for (although you know what they say about publicity!).

For a longer event, try to find a way to have something a little more substantial. It's safe to default to pizza, which is relatively inexpensive, easy to obtain, and universally appreciated. You may be able to get a discount or donation from a local store or a donation from your Friends of the Library or even from involved parents, but again, you really get a big return on this investment in terms of goodwill toward the organization. Also, if gamers get hungry, they're going to run out to get something, from the vending machines if you've got them or from nearby businesses if they exist, and it can result in missed matches and other disruptions. If you provide pizza, it's a good idea to have soda to go with it, but not essential.

You should plan to slowly mete out whatever food you have over the course of the event. Don't put out all the pretzels or cookies at the beginning. Plan to have the pizza delivered halfway through a longer event, and don't put out the soda until the pizza comes, offering only water up to the big moment. Don't get soda cans: they're too easily forgotten and replaced. You'll have better luck with small cups and two-liter bottles. You can provide markers and encourage players to mark their cups, which I've done with varying levels of success. In any case, this is going to make a mess, so just expect to clean it up at the end, throwing out half-full (is that still optimistic in this context?) cups, smashed goldfish in the carpet, gum wrappers, etc. It is a pain, but you should view it as the detritus of success and just be thankful that you don't have to clean up after them every day.

You must resist the urge to ask them to be neat. It won't have any impact on the amount of cleanup, and it can only undermine the good relationship you're working to build. Embrace the slovenliness. Remember that they can always go back home to their basements and nobody will hassle them there. Odds are that they are already expecting you to be fuddy-duddies; don't give them the satisfaction of being right.

The worst tournament war story I have regarding food is when the fifty-five pizzas were ninety minutes late to a five-hour tournament. As the hungry teens lined up hopefully, jockeying for position to pounce upon the first whiff of greasy cardboard that wafted their way, we announced that we had heard from the pizza place and that the driver had been hit by "a Mack truck" (he was very specific) en route to the library. The first question was, of course, "Are the pizzas OK?" They were, and the driver was too, and the precious sustenance ultimately arrived intact, and life went on.

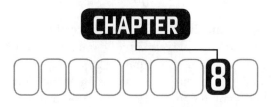

CHAPTER

8

Now What?

or How to Leverage the Interesting Smell You've Discovered

Pulling off a successful tournament event (or even one with some significant mishaps) is a major achievement, affecting the attendees' perceptions about you and your organization. However, you can realize even bigger benefits if you can take some steps outside the events to help the community that you've built continue and build some critical mass of its own. It increases the draw and the value of your service to the gamers, and it strengthens the audience and intensity of your next event. Helping this community grow online, and also finding other things you can do with it, will keep your gamers more enthusiastically involved in the organization and maximize the positive outcomes for the library.

8.1 Establishing an Online Home for Your Fans, or Building Geek Central

As your events catch on, build buzz, and earn devotees, a community will start to coalesce around your events. While there's plenty of benefit to having this community just coalesce once a month, you can keep the involvement going, add more value, and strengthen and mold the community identity if you're able to offer your players a place online where they can congregate to talk trash, complain, and hurl insults at each other. Sounds great, doesn't it?

This single step can do more to maximize the positive benefits for your organization and your players' involvement with you than any other. It can be a long time between tournaments, and if you can give them a place to think and talk about your events in those long, empty weeks, you'll get a higher level of commitment, more returning players, and simply more love for the library.

You can establish this online home with varying degrees of complexity. The simplest (and often the most effective) way would just be to create a free online blog at Blogger or a similar service for the purpose of promoting your tournaments and allow players to comment. You can do this without spending a dime or requiring the assistance of a single geek type: you can simply register and create mylibrarygaming.blogspot.com or the like for free (see section 5.6 for more) and start promoting that URL on your regular website, in any print materials, and most important, at your tournaments. Make posts to promote each event at least a week in advance and then post the results and voila: instant community. You can also use this format to announce tournament rules you're proposing and get feedback on them or to find out what games you should investigate and what times are best for your players. You may want to read through the history of the AADL service as shown in blog posts at www.aadl.org/aadlgt/.

Depending on what resources you have available, you may wish to use a different method to build community online; you can try more traditional web forums (who knew web forums were traditional already?), blogs on your library website, a MySpace for your tournament series, or even a chat room. The key is that you can talk to your audience, and they can talk back.

And talk back they will. There will be disagreements, there will be name-calling, and there will be inappropriate language. However, I've gotten to the point where I consider those things to be assets to the online community because they give me an opportunity to demonstrate to the players where the boundaries of acceptable behavior are without having to spell it out in another dreaded set of rules. This is your blog and your service; don't hesitate to tell a player publicly when they've stepped over the line, but be friendly and don't hold a grudge about it. I tend to expect players to be respectful and stay on topic, but I'm a lot more rigid about the former than the latter. However, you should expect and tolerate some trash talking. It's all part of the game, and if you do events for sixth through twelfth grade like we do, there will be an axis that cuts across the middle school and high school crowds with name-calling on both sides, especially when middle schoolers win things, which the high schoolers will attribute to the middle schoolers having less homework and thus more time to practice. Note that you do not have to listen to that argument with a straight face.

Be sure to promote your blog or forum at your events. Give out the URL and let players know what they can expect to find there. Let them know that it's the place where they can get information about upcoming tournaments, make suggestions for future tournaments, and so on. It's a good idea to come up with some participation ideas that are only online to give a strong incentive for players to get involved. I've done things like online commentary auditions and directing questions or suggestions about specific scoring minutiae online; it's a great way to attract players who may be coming to the events but aren't yet involved online.

The whole point is that the community that your events create is able to persist online, giving the players an opportunity to gab and strut as they may and giving you a chance to be a part of it. It's an Internet truth that no matter what you're into, people are talking about it online. Don't let your tournament series be an exception!

8.1.1   A Few Words on an Informal Blogging Voice and Its Benefits

Remember our image problem? Unfortunately, many players, especially the teens, are going to have certain expectations about the personalities and perceptions of someone who works at the public library, and often they ain't pretty. Keep that image of the shushing finger in mind as you're writing posts and endeavor to destroy that stereotype at every opportunity. Here's a list of dos and don'ts when blogging with your gaming audience:

DON'T call teens "kids" or even "teens" if you can avoid it.

DO call them "players" or "gamers" or, better yet, "rookies," "veterans," and "masters" where appropriate.

DON'T maintain any semblance of professional distance or write in the third person.

DO use lots of "I," "me," and "we," as long as it's not the royal we.

DON'T complain, even obliquely, about the resultant mess or hassle of a tournament. Complaining about the smell is OK, because they all assume it's not them.

DO feel free to fondly tease players about the filth if you simply must say something.

DON'T talk about reading, learning, school, or college.

DO make posts promoting other events your players might be interested in.

DON'T ask for feedback if you don't intend on changing your plans.

DO require positions to be supported by strong arguments.

DON'T allow an inappropriate comment to go by without a remark from you.

DO use a light touch to correct, "Sorry, but that last comment is over the line. Let's leave his momma out of this," and never lecture.

DON'T hide behind a handle or pseudonym.

DO just use your first name and *never* insist on Miss, Ms., or Mr.

With the right voice, you can allow that sense of community to build and establish a great rapport with your new fans. The key is to keep it light, informal, fun, and honest and to build excitement. Just like when you've got them in the room, look for the stories and the drama and build the excitement with each post.

8.1.2 Getting the Word Out Early, or Getting Worms (Like an Early Bird, Not a Stray Dog)

In chapter 5 we talked about word of mouth as the most effective marketing tool for reaching new users. That can start slowly, so you should build fermentation time into your promotion plans. However, getting the word out early to the community not only gives the buzz time to build but also gives busy players a better chance to be able to fit your events into their packed weekend schedules, especially during the school year. When you have a series planned, the sooner you can get the word out about the final tournament and its prizes, the sooner players will start to get the idea and get excited about their chances.

It's a good idea to make a post when you first set your schedule of tournaments for the next few months and then post on each event again a week or two before it happens. Don't hesitate to promote future events, even distant ones, on the mic during a tournament. It may seem that nobody will remember the specific date, and they won't, but they'll remember that the library is going to have a Guitar Hero tournament in October, and they'll find out the details later, and guess where that will lead them!

Another good thing you'll want to promote far in advance is when print brochures or handouts will be available, especially if they're in production. Let players know that they'll be able to pick up the spring brochure at the end of the month at the desk, and guess where that will lead them!

Also, announcing events far in advance, especially when they're around holiday breaks at school, gives your players a chance to influence family vacation plans to make sure that they'll be in town for the finals.

8.1.3 Answering Their Incessant Questions

Tournaments can be conceptually complex beasts. Combine that inherent complexity with a middle school boy's frequent distractedness and anxiety about measuring up to any nearby peer group, and you've got a formula to produce questions at a rate of 2.6 player questions per staff member per minute. (I counted once.) This will be at its peak during the tournament, when the leaderboard and its fundamental declarations of worth will keep them on edge and thirsty for information. But if you've got a good community going online, there will still be plenty of questions between tournaments about standings, scoring methods, when the next tournament is (even as a comment on a post that says when the next tournament is), how they can sign up, if anyone wants to play for money, and if anyone saw their black jacket after the last tournament.

First, don't feel that you have to respond to these online questions right away, especially if it's three weeks before your next tournament and they should just chill. A short response time does make a very positive impression, but it also doesn't hurt for some of your more intense or pushy players to understand that you have other responsibilities. Also, unless you're using threaded discussions, you don't need to respond to each question individually. When the questions are really flying I'll make a comment every four or five days answering all the new questions at once.

Don't feel that you need to have an answer about every minute detail of how you'll run the tournament. I know it doesn't come naturally to a librarian, but it's OK to say, "We don't know yet." It's always good to turn a question around, as, for instance, when you have no clue whether self-destructs will count for 0 or −1 in Super Smash Bros., especially since the answer is that you'll be awarding points based on finishing place, not kills. Ask them what they suggest, but make sure that it's clear that the final decision is yours.

As your community matures, you'll get a few righteous souls who will take up the heavy, heavy mantle of correcting all of these revolting n00bs who are ignorant of the intricacies of your gaming program, and they'll answer questions for you, and sometimes they'll even be right. When they're not, just step in with an "actually . . ." and your know-it-alls will stand quietly corrected or else start back in on their crusade to convince you to adopt whatever it was they just thought they knew.

You might consider a tournament wiki, if you're wikily inclined, and update it every time you answer one of those questions. However, that can rapidly lead to a much more fixed and cumbersome set of rules than if you just reserve the right to change the rules (fairly) when needed.

8.1.4 Cultivating Involvement, Buy-In, and Stalking

Allowing the community to continue online gives you an outstanding opportunity to get a higher level of involvement from your players, both in your tournaments and in the rest of the library. There will be a subset of your players who are just crazy about the whole thing, and they will want to be involved in everything that you will allow them, plus whatever they can get away with when you're not looking. It's a little trickier to get the more casual players involved.

The easiest way to get buy-in is to give them a chance to affect the decisions that go into the event and listen to what they say. It's still important to maintain that veto power (or perhaps employ signing statements) in case they get all excited about something unworkable logistically, financially, or politically, but see the next section for that.

The commentary booth (or table) is a great place to get high-quality participation from your players. At preseason tournaments I'll often do an open commentary mic to give all kinds of players a chance to try it, but it's also a bit of an audition to help decide who gets the job later. Combine that with an online written audition in the comments on a blog post, and you've got higher participation from all the hopefuls, even though you pick the geekiest (or rather, most geeked) ones.

If you've got a leaderboard, you could also consider involvement bonuses if you're having a hard time jump-starting online participation. Just be consistent with the size of the rewards (e.g., 100 points for a commentary audition or a suggestion for prizes) and know when you've outgrown the incentive.

Along these lines, involvement premiums or food are surefire ways to get better attendance at focus groups or planning meetings (see section 8.3). We've given out DVDs of the previous grand championships, T-shirts, or even just a bag of pretzels at planning meetings, and having open play doesn't hurt either.

You'll also probably get players showing up early—as much as *two hours* early, just poking around and wondering if they can help set up (or hanging around and seeing if they can help take down). Once you get to know your players, this can be a great way to decrease the time or staff needed for setup. You can also call on your trusted players to help reset the LAN if it goes down during a match or if you need to do a game switch in the middle of a tournament. They'll usually have seen you do it so many times they know just what to do.

With your newfound celebrity status, you may even find yourself with a superfan: someone who comes early and stays late every time and is maybe even a little aggressive and stubborn about suggesting ways they can help you out. It's always hard to say no to such earnestly geeked-out fanboys, but you can't let them helpfully push you around either. If they step over the nuisance line, don't hesitate to let them know it and that they'll have to earn your trust back. Then say no to the next three things they ask you if they can do. When you then welcome them back into the fold, they'll get the message.

8.2 Questions You Should Ask Them, and When It's OK to Ignore the Answers

Your tournament series is the sum of the decisions you make as you're designing the service. Especially if you're not a thumb wiggler yourself, these decisions can seem impossibly arcane, technical, or even obtuse. If you don't know for sure what you want to do, there's no better way to design a patron-oriented service than to let the patrons orient the service. You can ask them what games you should play, what accessories you should buy, what tournament format you should use, what the prizes should be, or anything else that comes up. There's just one question you should never, ever, ever ask them, no matter how badly you want to know the answer: never, ever ask what console they think you should buy.

This one issue easily accounts for a significant percentage of all the arguing on the entire Web. Because a console may often represent a first large investment by an adolescent boy, or even be representative of the entire household's with-it-ness, fanboys really, really want to feel good about the choice they made when they bought their chosen console, and put simply, everything else sucks. Do not get involved in this conversation, especially when you haven't yet bought any hardware; you'll instantly alienate part of your audience no matter what you choose if they feel that you ignored their recommendation on this most schismatic of choices.

That's why, as mentioned above in chapter 3, you should keep the conversation focused on the software. Find out what they really want to play and choose the hardware that gives you the most options. However, whenever you ask them questions, especially this one, give clear boundaries to the acceptable answers. If you're not going to consider any M-rated games, lay that out as you're asking the question. If you've already made hardware decisions, or if you only want to take games that support LAN mode or maybe just four simultaneous players, just give them the parameters they need to consider.

With those decisions behind you, you have all the tournament decisions to make. Excellent questions to ask players are what modes of the chosen game should be used in events or how the prizes should be awarded. Most of the suggestions will be very fair-minded and thoughtful, but don't hesitate to make them defend their suggestions if you have concerns, or simply shoot down ideas with fatal flaws (like a round-robin tournament for eighty-three players). Working through this online will really help build buy-in and cut down on complaints later and can be a lifesaver if you don't know where to begin.

If you're going to use a scoring system, definitely make a post about it in advance so that your players can run through all the scenarios they're worried about and make sure that your system scores fairly in the most obscure situations. For example, here are some more questions you should and should not ask your burgeoning community:

DO ask if they'd rather have qualification rounds or a single-elimination tournament.

DON'T ask that if you don't want to mess with qualification rounds.

DO ask what stores they might like to see gift card prizes from.

DON'T ask how much each prize should be.

DO ask what games or genres they'd like to play in tournaments.

DON'T ask which console is the best of them all.

DO ask what day of the week or time of day works best for them.

DON'T ask how often you should have gaming events.

DO ask how many points they should get for first place, especially in a multitournament season.

DON'T ask how many players they think should get into the finals.

DO ask where they think you should promote your events and what they think of your fliers.

DON'T ask what the fliers should look like, unless you're ready for them to produce and distribute their own!

Again, remember that you are in charge here, and you reserve the right to not take their suggestions. However, you should try to respond to every suggestion, and if you don't plan on adopting it, tell them why, even if it's just, "I don't want to get into that yet." Similarly, be sure to let them know when you've been convinced and recognize those strong arguments publicly to demonstrate what it takes to change your mind.

A lot of this assumes that you have your community rolling before you even have an event, and while that can happen, it's more likely that your online community will experience the most growth when you're able to promote it during a successful event, a bit of cart and horse syndrome. However, if you're getting the word out in advance, the fact that you're offering an opportunity for players to influence the formation of the service can be a real added draw during the start-up phase, and you can still get excellent feedback from an online community that only has three or four active members. I guess that would be more of a cadre, maybe even a cabal if they all agreed on everything. Like that would happen.

8.3 Focus Groups, Panels, and Other Unnatural Settings for Teenagers

While the feedback you get online can help you fine-tune your programs, you should also consider doing a meeting every once in a while to sort through some of the big questions with your hard-core players. This makes particular sense if you're doing seasons, as you can do a preseason meeting or a postseason wrap-up to talk about how your service should evolve into its next incarnation. Many libraries have Teen Advisory Board traditions of varying vitality, so there's certainly a precedent, but having a meeting just about where to take your tournaments next can bring new energy and ideas into the building.

However, you may need to bribe them as mentioned in section 8.1.4 to get them through the door. Premiums, swag, and food can help, but nothing's going to get them in like open play. If you're considering new games for your next cycle, you may also use this opportunity to allow the players to bring in their own (E- or T-rated) games that they'd like to see in the future. Plan a three-hour event and talk for about the last hour or so.

It will really help to have an agenda and get it into their hands ahead of time via your blog. That way they'll have a chance to prepare their positions and all that stuff. You need to have a good grasp on the questions you want to get answered during the meeting and keep things moving, since there will invariably be ruts that everyone gets stuck in. You'll likely need to police who has the floor once things get rolling (conch anyone?), and I can tell you that I've had to raise my voice on occasion to get the discussion back under control. I even had to issue a single loud clap once to get their attention back, but I acknowledge that I'm a loud clapper.

Anyway, if you get a good crowd, these can be very positive and fun events, especially when done between seasons, because everyone but last season's champion will be highly interested in changing things to their advantage. Again, like a conversation on your blog, you'll get the most out of it if you pitch ideas for them to respond to instead of having to give everyone an opportunity to riff on what bugged them about last season.

We call these events "Game and Plan Meet-Ups," and we try to avoid words like "teen," "advisory," and "board" because they sound either lame or suspiciously like work. Be sure to promote these meetings at your tournaments (focusing on the open play elements) to try to maximize your turnout.

In addition to the focus group–style event, you can also build your community through panel discussions about games or a dedicated format "to finally settle the issue of which console is the best," with your players as the panelists. However, these events are typically not a huge draw for your gamer audience, and even if you get a good panel together, there's the risk that no audience will show up. It's something to think about as your community grows.

8.4 Getting and Keeping Momentum, like a Luge or Something

You want your tournaments to grow and take on a life of their own. You want the expectations of your players to be ever increasing and for them to never wonder for a moment if your service will continue. Once you start reaching that new audience and getting the ball rolling, there are a few things you should consider as you plan that can help you build momentum for your service and keep it moving.

The simplest way to keep the momentum is to piggyback on the annual rhythm of a teenager's life and structure your events in annual seasons. That way they'll always know when the next season is starting, and the way it fits into their lives over the year will rapidly become familiar, from the August tournaments that conflict with band camp to the December championships that make them want to stay home from family vacations.

Having that season in half the year also defines your off-season when you'll have more flexibility about whether or not to schedule tournaments without failing to meet their expectations. The major point to consider is that you should always know, at least roughly, when the next event will be. At the beginning of your season, you should have the rest of the season and championships planned out; when you get to the championships, you should have your off-season schedule together. There should always be something definitely upcoming, even if it's three months away, for them to look forward to and to help cement the service in their minds as something that's here to stay.

As your momentum builds, there may well be a time when your growth plateaus (and that may be just fine with you). At AADL we've used recruitment point bonuses to good effect to keep growing and to take advantage of the viral nature of word-of-mouth campaigns, including an offer of 500 points to a clan with a new player in it or 1,000 points to a clan with a *girl* in it! These sorts of tricks don't cost anything, but they really deliver. Another thing you can do if you offer clans is to use clan rankings to break ties, meaning members of higher-ranked clans advance. This really encourages clan participation, especially among the players who lost a tiebreaker because they weren't affiliated with a clan at all.

Another good technique to keep momentum is to reinforce the cyclical nature of your service when you're emcee and in your promotions, using phrases like, "The biggest tournament series in town is back for another season," "See you next year," or "This could be their breakout season." Just letting the players hear you talk about next season cements its relevance and importance in their minds and makes them more likely than ever before to seek out your promotional materials.

Finally, you can sustain your momentum through to your postseason planning meetings or open play focus groups by using that as your stock answer to complaints or criticisms: "Well, just come to our planning meet-up in February and maybe you can convince us." Let them know that they will have that opportunity to make a big impact on the direction of the service next season and what they can do during the off-season to prepare!

8.5 Impact on Other Library Services, or Throw Them a Bone, Then Run

A common, tremulously asked question in the public library world is what if it works? We could be besieged by people who want things that we have! I guess that's the difference between us and the for-profit sector. They're not afraid of smash-hit success. We shouldn't be either, but it's hard to let go of the relative (and yet ominous) peace and quiet of the reference desk and dive into the throngs. Once you've got the throngs, though, what else can be done with them, and how can you keep them coming back for more? What exactly is the ante, and how can it be upped?

8.5.1 The Halo Effect. No, Not That Halo.

While I don't consider videogame events to be a loss leader (what, haven't you been paying attention?), bringing this new audience into the building and showing them that you respect them and their pastimes can indeed lead to more of them showing up at other events and using other services that the library has to offer. We've seen our players entering short stories in writing contests, showing up at anime events, sushi demonstrations, Claymation workshops, and book discussions, and even occasionally asking questions at the reference desk. One of our earliest players once described videogame events as "a gateway drug for libraries."

You can help this along by gently promoting your other events at tournaments, but it's advisable not to push the more bookish stuff too hard. Just give them a flier that includes the other events. Be aware that you can undo the goodwill you earn by overemphasizing the school-related stuff at a tournament.

Similarly, you can help gamers discover your collections by scattering the good, light stuff, like manga and gaming magazines, around the room during an event, but again, avoid anything with a library binding or even any hardcover for that matter. They will discover your collections, and they will check them out; you just have to let it happen on its own. Horse to water and all that.

However, with this audience in hand, you may be able to take another shot at events that didn't deliver on previous attempts but may be easier to promote to a gaming audience, like collectible card game events or other equally dorky pursuits. You can also try a rock-paper-scissors tournament. Seriously. They're fantastically fun and a bull's-eye for the already hypercompetitive gaming audience.

It's a good approach just to let the halo effect happen and then intensify your promotional resources around the events and services that get the most glow and that you know are the most appealing to your gaming audience. I've gone around the building after a tournament debriefing staff at different desks to find out where the players were wandering around during the event and what else they were doing.

Finally, there may be some spillover that will surprise you. For example, we had a player once who lost a high-pressure tiebreaker at the championships and took it really hard. He decided he was going to go upstairs and read some Piers Anthony to try to calm down. Later a finalist disappeared, so we dispatched another player to go find the reader and bring him back down for his second chance. He went on to win fourth prize that day. He must have been reading the Adept series, am I right?

8.5.2   Expanding Your Audience, or It's Not Just for Fanboys Anymore

While much of your early success may well come from relatively hard-core gamers, who are usually a new audience for libraries, there is a lot of potential to expand the audience of your gaming events beyond that hard-core crowd, reaching not only back into your traditional patrons but also out to less fervent gamers in the community.

The rhythm and physical games are great for this, especially if you can do them someplace where passersby can see. Many of these games are compelling to wide audiences, and if you can create that safe space for people to try them, you'll get moms, dads, and even grandparents trying them out and having fun. Karaoke Revolution is great for this too. Also, the breakthrough fun of the Wii opens up some possibilities for attracting audiences to gaming events that they wouldn't have considered before.

You can jump-start this process by having events that are intended exclusively for intergenerational audiences, like a DDR tournament for parent-child teams, or just by having separate brackets for older players so that they don't have to compete against the whippersnappers.

Retro games can also tap into adult nostalgia and get new players through the door; we've had some unexpected faces at our retro events. Other more casual game events, like perhaps a Bejeweled tournament, can tap into some other game players who wouldn't have interest in a fighting game or a shooter.

You may want to consider trying to hit all the audiences each time you set up your equipment; that's one of the chief advantages of a tournament weekend. You can have three different events for different audiences and get the most out of that setup time. Also, if you have, for example, a fighting game tournament for teens and up Friday night, then a big season event for teens on Saturday, and an all-ages DDR tourney on Sunday, not only is there something for everyone, but the hard-core teens can come to all three events.

Finally, if you start with console games, there's always the possibility of branching out into LAN parties or other events for PC gamers, usually an older, more serious demographic. As the gaming audience continues to grow, so will your events and the demand for different approaches and games.

8.5.3 Gaming Elements in Other Programs

You'll quickly discover how much participation competitive elements can engender; why not allow those gaming elements to spread to other programs? Libraries often strive to make summer reading games noncompetitive, but why does it have to be that way? What kind of completion rate might you get if there was a leaderboard? You can also use this approach to entice your gaming audience to participate in events you do in partnership with other institutions, like point bonuses for off-site tournaments or targeted recruitment bonuses (1,000 points for every YMCA member in your clan), although those can seem a little cheap.

You can also just directly add gaming into other events. We always set up the DDR pads at our anime events just to increase the available options. You can also look for other places that open plays might be welcomed: as part of partnerships, during events for younger kids that teens may be dragged to, or opposite school functions they may wish to avoid.

8.6 To Infinity, and Beyond!

Once you've reached out to gamers, welcomed them into your organization, and demonstrated that their leisure choices are valid inside your brick-and-mortar walls, the sky's the limit to what you can do with this passionate and fanatical audience. Gaming events are a logical next step for the public library, and they continue our evolution and pursuit of something for everyone. The gaming audience is growing bigger (and older) every day. Starting a gaming service at your library is a key to your organization's maintaining its relevance as the cherished rugs are pulled out from under libraries, one after another.

The most important thing in my experience is to take the opportunity to forge a completely nonpedantic and mutually appreciative relationship with teenagers and show them that it's their library too. As they grow up and become passionate superpatrons, who knows what they'll expect of us and how much they'll be willing to do to help us achieve it?

I've made my case for why videogames belong in public libraries, what form your gaming service can take, and how you can make it happen at any scale; now it's up to you to push Start. Just remember that every boss has a weak spot, every puzzle has a solution, and if you lose a life, you can always continue.

How high can you get?

CHAPTER 9

Links, Resources, and Even a Book or Two

OK, you've heard my choice 65,000 words on the topic; now you'd probably like a second opinion. Of course, there are lots of resources out there about the cultural impact of games, the positive benefits, and the latest news, and there are other libraries that have had phenomenal success with their gaming programs. Here's more information on the topic.

9.1 Other Books to Consider, Probably without So Many Borderline Naughty Words

Simulations and the Future of Learning: An Innovative (and Perhaps Revolutionary) Approach to e-Learning, by Clark Aldrich

The Kids Are Alright: How the Gamer Generation Is Changing the Workplace, by John C. Beck and Mitchell Wade

Smartbomb: The Quest for Art, Entertainment, and Big Bucks in the Videogame Revolution, by Heather Chaplin and Aaron Ruby

Recreational Games and Tournaments: The Organisation of Small- and Intermediate-Sized Events, by Paul De Knop and Marny Theeboom

Game On: Gaming at the Library, by Beth Gallaway (forthcoming)

What Video Games Have to Teach Us about Learning and Literacy, by James Paul Gee

Why Video Games Are Good for Your Soul, by James Paul Gee

Everything Bad Is Good for You, by Steven Johnson

The Ultimate History of Video Games: From Pong to Pokémon—The Story behind the Craze That Touched Our Lives and Changed the World, by Steven L. Kent

Power-Up: How Japanese Video Games Gave the World an Extra Life, by Chris Kohler

Library Technology Reports: Intersection of Services, by Jenny Levine

"Don't Bother Me Mom—I'm Learning!" by Marc Prensky

Play between Worlds: Exploring Online Game Culture, by T. L. Taylor

9.2 Must-Read Websites, a Few of Which Will Make It Past a Filter

digg.com/gaming_news/: Gaming news links from around the Web

www.gamefaqs.com: Everything you want to know about every game; includes detailed LAN FAQs for LAN-supporting games

www.gamerankings.com: Indexed, summarized reviews of every game with links from around the gaming press

gamerdad.com: News and community for gamer parents

www.joystiq.com: Second-tier game blog

kotaku.com: Top game blog with daily impenetrable news

libgaming.blogspot.com: Gaming in libraries blog run by gaming goddess Beth Gallaway

www.libsuccess.org: Library best practices wiki (check the gaming page for detailed info about libraries doing gaming events)

www.penny-arcade.com: Thrice-weekly, foulmouthed gaming comic, with millions of readers

www.wikipedia.org: An excellent source for information about videogames

9.3 Game-Specific Fansites

www.ddrfreak.com: Fan central for DDR; includes forums to announce tournaments

forum.guitarherogame.com: Official forum for Guitar Hero series

maddenplanet.com: Madden fansite

mario-kart.net: Mario Kart fansite

planethalo.gamespy.com: Halo fan central

smashboards.com: The smash world forums; fan central for Super Smash Bros.

soulcalibur.com: Official site for Soul Calibur; includes fan forums

9.4 Game Industry Sites

www.esrb.org: Detailed information about game ratings and a complete searchable database of games by rating

gamasutra.com: Industry news site with highly professional reporting

theesa.com: The Entertainment Software Association; home to many useful facts and figures

9.5 Game Stuff Vendors

www.BracketMaker.com: Free, flexible online bracket generator

cableorganizer.com: Great source for Velcro ties, cable covers, and sleeving

cobaltflux.com: Makers of high-end, extremely durable dance pads

markertek.com: Professional audio and video vendor, with huge catalog and good reps

www.milestek.com: Great source for cables and S-Video baluns

redoctane.com: Manufacturer of dance pads and guitar controllers; offers simple event sponsorships

trophycentral.com: Source for supercheap custom trophies

9.6 Other Big Library Gaming Programs

Illinois—Bloomington Public Library, www.bngamefest.org

Kansas—Johnson County Public Library, www.jocolibrary.org/gaming/

North Carolina—Public Libraries of Charlotte and Mecklenberg County, thegamingzone.blogspot.com; large Soul Calibur tournaments; includes player-made commercials

South Carolina—Georgetown County Library System, Carvers Bay High School gaming club

Washington—King County Library System, kcls.org/teens/gameon.cfm

INDEX

A genuine gaming geek who became hooked on his first Atari console at age five, Eli Neiburger piloted and runs a string of successful gaming tournaments at Ann Arbor District Library, where he is the technology manager. He has presented gaming talks and workshops at a variety of conferences around the country. When he's not at the library, he and his wife are proudly schooling (and being schooled by) their five-year-old son, Nemo, and toddler daughter, Rocket, in the subtleties of Mario Kart. In his private moments, Eli can be found playing classic Nintendo tunes on his clarinet or accordion.